8/93

D0554090

PRESENTING

William
Sleator

TUSAS 594

Twayne's United States Authors Series
Young Adult Authors

Patricia J. Campbell, General Editor

The Young Adult Authors books seek to meet the
need for critical studies of fiction for young adults.
Each volume examines the life and work of one
author, helping both teachers and readers of young
adult literature to understand better the writers they
have read with such pleasure and fascination.

PRESENTING

William
Sleator

James E. Davis
and
Hazel K. Davis

Twayne Publishers • New York
Maxwell Macmillan Canada • Toronto
Maxwell Macmillan International • New York   Oxford   Singapore   Sydney

*To our thousands of students everywhere,
most of whom have also been our teachers.*

Presenting William Sleator
James E. Davis and Hazel K. Davis

Photographs kindly provided by William Sleator.

Twayne Publishers   Maxwell Macmillan Canada, Inc.
Macmillan Publishing Company   1200 Eglinton Avenue East
866 Third Avenue   Suite 200
New York, NY 10022   Don Mills, Ontario M3C 3N1

Macmillan Publishing Company is part of the Maxwell Communication
Group of Companies

10 9 8 7 6 5 4 3 2 1

The paper used in this publication meets the minimum requirements
of American National Standard for Information Sciences—Permanence
of Paper for Printed Library Materials, ANSI Z39.48-1984. ∞"

Printed and bound in the United States of America.

Library of Congress Cataloging-in-Publication Data

Davis, James E., 1934–
    Presenting William Sleator / James E. Davis and Hazel K. Davis.
        p.   cm. — (Twayne United States authors series: TUSAS
    594. Young adult authors)
    Includes bibliographical references and index.
    ISBN 0-8057-8215-X:
    1. Sleator, William—Criticism and interpretation. 2. Young adult
fiction, American—History and criticism. [1. Sleator, William—
Criticism and interpretation. 2. American literature—History and
criticism.] I. Davis, Hazel K., 1941– . II. Title.
III. Series: Twayne United States authors series; TUSAS 594.
IV. Series: Twayne United States authors series. Young adult
authors.
PS3569.L353Z65 1991
813'.54—dc20   91-31933
                                                                CIP

Contents

Preface

Make the book interesting. . . . Give adolescents something that they want to read . . . then try to make it literature. But first, make them *want* to read it.

— William Sleator

William Sleator puts his own directive into practice with characters and situations that have made his readers want to read him since his first book was published in 1970, but especially so since *House of Stairs* appeared in 1974. His almost-ordinary adolescents are placed into challenging or even threatening situations, usually involving what he calls "nutty paradoxes," and the results are not always predictable. In *House of Stairs* Sleator puts six teenagers into a maze of stairs where every nuance of behavior and bodily function can be observed by not only those trapped in the maze but by the unseen experimenters as well. In later books his characters are faced with such devices as an egg enabling its possessor to travel back and forth in time, a duplicating machine that produces clones of the user, a spot in an Iowa field where time is sped up, an invasion of earth by game-playing creatures from outer space, and a sophisticated time-travel device whose use may lead to absolute chaos and the end of the world. His three children's books also contain seemingly ordinary children who are able to actually enter the world they have just drawn on paper, who can have their wishes granted by a doll's head, and who suddenly shrink and become part of the life in a doll's house, as well as a girl whose lies have caused her banishment from her original world to earth. The reader is led to wonder what if these things could really happen, if one could read a friend's mind, if time travel really were possible: "What would I do?"

Sleator says he has always been fascinated by time travel, which he calls a nonverifiable, totally impossible concept that he "clings to." On the dust jacket for *The Green Futures of Tycho* he is quoted as saying, "What I love is the freedom, greater than flying; also the mastery over fate that time travel would provide." He admits the concept is "rife with nutty paradoxes, some of which I have tried to explain in this book."[1]

Our desire to find out more about Sleator's "nutty paradoxes" led us to meet him, listen to him speak, and arrange various conversations with him beginning in 1984 at the Youngstown (Ohio) State University English Festival. In other contacts by letter and phone the subject of a possible book was discussed. His willingness, even enthusiasm, for the project spurred us on, and since our marathon discussion in his Boston home in 1987, we have never regretted getting to know William Sleator and his works as fully as possible.

Sleator began his career by writing the text for *The Angry Moon*, a Caldecott Honor Book. Other children's works include *Among the Dolls, That's Silly,* and *Once, Said Darlene. Blackbriar* and *Run* are books in which he has set places he has lived into mysterious, bizarre plots. With *House of Stairs* he ventured into science fiction and has been there ever since (with the exception of *Fingers*). He always deals with believable human characters, usually intelligent, well-read, sensitive young adults. He is a master at making the complex and intricate seem clear.

Always willing to talk to both teachers and their students about his craft in such settings as individual classrooms, young writers' conferences, conventions, assemblies, and interviews, Sleator does not just breeze in, do his thing, and leave. He listens to others and fully participates. He answers questions from the audience quite truthfully and stresses that writing is *work*. "Being creative isn't some type of magical thing at all. It is work, just like any kind of work," Sleator says.

Public speaking gets him out of the isolation of writing and gives him immediate direct response from audiences. His enthusiasm for speaking shows clearly when he says, "There is no feeling like getting up in front of a large group of people and making them laugh; it is a real high. I found out that I am a ham, and this is a great way to express this side of me."

Sleator enjoys hearing from his readers. He says, "A lot of the letters I get are from kids who are juvenile delinquents who respond to these characters and to these books and situations. They all tell me that my books are weird and I think, 'Good, good.'" He does not, however, approve of students writing to him just because of a class assignment: "I feel a lot of hassle with this, like I'm supposed to be helping them do their assignments. I don't want to do that." He feels the reward should be in the reading of a book. "Give them a book that is fun to read. That's my main concern," he says.

All Sleator's lead characters have typical problems for their ages, such as sibling rivalry, or difficulty relating to a parent, older person, or a peer. His characters, however, are not quite ordinary. He says he "thinks about characters in terms of people who don't fit into the stereotypes, who are different." He wants teenagers to feel empathy toward those who are different and "to try to act on that understanding." He says he trys to "focus on relationships, how people trust other people. . . . If you are going to have the reader believe, you've got to make it convincing—even if it's true."[2]

Sleator has said there might be an "alien influence" on his work, inspiring him to create his bizarre plots. He likes to write science fiction/fantasy because it enables his readers to live out fantasies they could not do otherwise. As Dr. Jerome L. Singer has pointed out in *The Inner World of Daydreaming* and *The Child's World of Make Believe,* the fuller a child's fantasy life, the more effectively that child can cope with real life. Sleator says, "It is very useful and practical to put yourself mentally in another time and place when you are sitting in a traffic jam or waiting in line at the supermarket."[3] Revenge fantasies are much better than actually taking revenge. Sleator speculates that readers of science fiction, because of their rich fantasy lives, are less likely to commit crimes. He says, "A lot of the fun of writing science fiction is learning about real phenomena. . . . The challenge is to try to make the parts you invent as believable as the scientific laws you are using. If you succeed, then you are giving the reader something that is magical and fantastic but at the same time might actually be possible. That's the greatest thing about science fiction—*someday it could really happen.*"[4]

Candid about his books, Sleator says: "By the time my books are published I am bored with working on them. I rarely sit down and read my books after they're published. I get a feeling of satisfaction of seeing it there with the nice jacket art, flipping through the pages. And it's even more satisfying when you get a good intelligent review, when somebody sees what you're trying to do" (Roginski, 202). He thinks his books are positive and that even though ugly things happen, they end happily: "It's more fun to read a book where maybe a lot of horrible things happen and at the end something good happens. And when you close the book you have a feeling of satisfaction" (Roginski, 201). These are the kinds of books he strives to write. Fortunately, Sleator is not nearly so sensitive now as he used to be about bad reviews. They don't bother him, or so he says. He handles it this way: "I just tell myself the critic is stupid—though, of course, I believe what I read in good reviews." Part of his confidence is the knowledge that kids really do like his books, no matter what adult critics may say.

We are indebted to William Sleator for his hours of interview time, his voluminous correspondence with us, his loan of family photographs, and his encouragement. Almost all the information in the first chapter of this book came from him. All comments from Sleator and quotations otherwise not credited are from his letters to us or from interviews. And we cannot thank Ann Durell, his editor at E. P. Dutton, enough. Her response by phone and her long letter to us about the editing of each manuscript make, we think, one of the most interesting features of this book. All quotations from her come from that letter, and we appreciate her permission to use them.

Chronology

1973 *Run.*

1974 Works as company pianist for the Boston Ballet Company, doing so until 1983. *House of Stairs.*

1975 *Among the Dolls.* Collaborates with Ron Cunningham on the ballet *Saturday Morning* for the Boston Ballet Company.

1976 *Take Charge: A Personal Guide to Behavior Modification* (with William H. Redd). Collaborates with Ron Cunningham on the ballet *Incident at Blackbriar* for the Boston Ballet Company.

1977 Collaborates with Ron Cunningham on the ballet *Minoan Dances* for the Boston Ballet Company.

1979 *Into the Dream. Once, Said Darlene.*

1981 *The Green Futures of Tycho. That's Silly.*

1982 Tours Europe with the Boston Ballet Company.

1983 *Fingers.* Leaves the Boston Ballet Company.

1984 *Interstellar Pig.*

1985 *Singularity.*

1986 *The Boy Who Reversed Himself.* Visits Thailand for the first time.

1987 Travels in Tuscany and Greece in the summer and lectures in Thailand.

1988 *The Duplicate.* Lectures in Thailand.

1989 "The Elevator," short story. Wins California Young Reader's Medal for *Interstellar Pig.*

1990 *Strange Attractors.*

1. William Sleator:
Ahead of Time from Birth

Early Life

"If you hadn't been premature you'd be really smart," William Sleator III's mother jokingly told him recently. Bill weighed only three and a half pounds when he was born prematurely on 13 February 1945 at Havre de Grace, Maryland. His mother, who worked as a contract surgeon at the health service for the army installation at Aberdeen, wore her unaltered army uniform until the end of her pregnancy. Her superior officer did not believe her at first when she told him she was going to the hospital to have a baby. Bill's father was doing research on ballistics at the Aberdeen proving grounds. When the baby was two months old, his parents took him to see Franklin Delano Roosevelt's funeral train; like many of the mourners, he wept. By the time Bill was three the family had moved to a suburb of St. Louis, Missouri, where Sleator spent his childhood. His father, William Warner Sleator, Jr., is a professor of physiology, and his mother, Esther Kaplan Sleator, is a pediatrician.

His parents' house was full of books and music. The four children—Bill was the oldest—were allowed to read whatever they wanted. Sleator remembers reading as a child the autobiography of Salvador Dali; he especially enjoyed the chapter titled "Intra-uterine Memories." He says, "I was one of those people who just loved to read. I just loved words from the beginning. There was no question about it, no problem. All this reading was the best thing in the world. If only everyone was like that." Some of the writers whose work Sleator particularly admires are E. M. Forster, Muriel Spark, John Collier, Rumer Godden, and Robert Louis Stevenson.

His paternal grandmother, a Greek scholar, enjoyed reading books in the original Greek. Recalls Sleator:

> When she was in her eighties she would finish the dinner dishes and then sit down by the fire and open up Aristophanes in Greek and read it. That was her bedtime reading. That's what my father's family was like—they came to this country soon after 1620, and were scholars for generations—my great-grandmother was one of the first women to graduate from the University of Michigan. My mother's parents, in contrast, were poor and uneducated Jewish immigrants from the Warsaw ghetto who came to this country in 1910. Her father was a tailor, and they lived above his store. My mother was the first person in her family to graduate from high school—and then she went on to work her way through college and medical school, which was less common for a woman in the 1930s than it is today. My father's father, a physicist, was delighted that his son married a Jewish woman, partly because of his awareness of the great contributions Jews had made to science.

Sleator says his mother is a very strong woman and has been a major influence in his life. As well as being a pediatrician she is also an excellent photographer, one who had taken most of the photographs used on the dust jackets of his books and in other promotional materials.

Bill played the piano and wrote stories as a child. He learned to type as a five-year-old. The first story he remembers (written at age six) was called "The Fat Cat": "Once there was a fat cat. Boy was she fat. Well, not that fat. But pretty fat." He says even then he needed an editor. He took piano lessons for 12 years and played cello for 5. Bill showed an early interest in the grotesque. One of his first musical compositions was called "Guillotines in the Springtime." Even a school assignment to write a story about a holiday was turned into "The Haunted Easter Egg."

A Musical Family

Although he loved music and took to it eagerly, Sleator also points out that it was not a choice: "It was just an accepted fact in our family that all the kids would study musical instruments. It was not that our parents wanted us to become professional musicians—far from it, they wanted us to be university professors." It was simply that they believed their children's lives would be richer if they had the ability to play music for the pleasure of it— which turned out to be true. They proved it by example. Bill's father played in an amateur string quartet that would meet at their house. Some of Bill's happiest memories are of going to sleep while listening to beautiful live music being played downstairs. He says his parents were right not to give the children a choice about it, "because I think most kids don't know what's good for them, and the time to learn an instrument is when you are a child. A lot of kids wouldn't learn how to read if they weren't forced to, and the same is true of music. I can't imagine what it would be like not to be able to play the piano." When the family gets together now they play chamber music. Sleator's father plays the violin and viola, his brother Danny plays the viola, his brother Tycho plays the cello, and his sister, Vicky, plays the piano. The only one who doesn't play is their mother, who did not have the good fortune to be forced to learn an instrument as a child. When Bill's parents were first married, his mother made a valiant stab at learning cello. "Then," he says, "I was born. When I was an infant, every time she tried to approach the instrument I would shriek. Not because I didn't like the sound of it—I just couldn't stand to have her pay attention to anything except me."

High School Days

In high school in University City, Missouri, Bill liked his English teachers and says they had a major positive influence on his life: "It was an excellent public school system—my mother used to say that was because the community was largely Jewish, and so education was considered a top priority." He continued writing fiction and poetry, and, of course, he continued composing music as well. he loved the idea that people thought he was a genius when one of his compositions was played by the school orchestra in assembly. Sleator recalls, "When the piece was over I could see, from where I was sitting onstage in the cello section, certain kids in the audience getting up to give the piece a standing ovation—kids who not long before had made fun of me for being an oddball and lousy athlete. That memory has stuck with me."

As a teenager Bill was an outsider at first, not interested in sports. His sister, who was in the class below him, was involved in the popular clique for a while and Bill felt left out: "But during high school, we both began to collect other oddballs around us, and soon we had our own clique—we were the first hippies at University City High." They had long hair and wore oversized sweaters, ragged jeans haphazardly patched, long tie-dyed skirts from India, and leather sandals, and they carried army surplus backpacks for book bags. They were a small group at first but eventually swelled to include more than 100 kids. They even had their own car in the homecoming parade. All the other kids had shiny Cadillacs decorated with crepe paper, and they drove around the track in letter sweaters, waving pom-poms. Bill's group wore turtlenecks and reclined on a dented black wreck that had slogans like "God Is Dead" and "Life Is Absurd" painted on it.

When Bill was a senior in high school, he worked with a group to make an original motion picture, with help from an English teacher and from the art teacher, who had taken a course in cinematography. In 1963, long before video cameras, making a film was an unusual project for high school students. They got together and wrote the script, and then filmed it, chopped up the work print into hundreds of scenes, and edited it. Editing it, putting the scenes together, deciding on the order, and switching from one angle to another were the most interesting parts to Bill. The movie, called *The Magic Chalk,* was about three little boys who find a piece of chalk, and whatever they draw with it seems to happen to them in a sinister way. Sleator says:

> My little brothers were the stars, and my mother and father
> and I also had parts in the movie. My brother Danny, who was
> eight at the time, was old enough to do a lot of conscious acting,
> and he was great at it. My other brother, Tycho, who was six,
> was not consciously acting—we would just tell him what to do
> and see how it looked. In one scene, he was supposed to look
> up and see a statue of a lion, and get really excited. But for
> several takes he wouldn't get excited, he wouldn't look in the
> right direction, he got bored and began to sulk. Finally, Vicky
> and I stood behind the camera, and when the camera started
> rolling we suddenly shouted at Tycho and started making all
> sorts of obscene gestures at him. He lifted his head and his face
> lit up in a beautiful smile of innocent rapture.

It was one of the best shots in the film. Ironically, the only person
in the family who did not appear in the movie was Vicky, who,
according to Sleator, was a real beauty and very photogenic. Bill
wrote the musical score for the movie, of course—a score for
piano, flute, oboe, trumpet, and double bass. He enjoyed writing
movie music because of the limitation—the music has to fit the
scene exactly, to the second. He also liked the fact that the music
sets the emotional tone of the scene—the same footage can be
made to seem funny or tragic, depending on the music.

"In high school I was the dumbest one in the accelerated science
and math classes," Sleator says bluntly. As a senior he enrolled in
calculus. It was tough for him, and he was busy with all those
extracurricular activities like *The Magic Chalk*. He also wrote a
ballet to Poe's "The Masque of the Red Death," performed at an
evening program by the modern dance classes. Sleator says, "My
father's aunt and uncle, both famous scientists, came to see it. My
great-aunt, an interesting character who had been a flapper in
the twenties, laughed throughout the entire performance." Because Bill was so busy, a good friend, who was an English teacher,
suggested he drop out of calculus, since he would never need it,
and take a study hall to have more time. His father objected, but
he dropped out anyway. Years later he was to regret this decision.

Of his growing up Sleator says: "There was a certain amount of
pressure on us to excel. My parents expected us all to be brilliant.
Though I did all this creative stuff, I was not the greatest student,
and often I felt like I was not good enough." His characters ex-

press those same feelings of inadequacy which he felt as a teen-ager. He says, "How do you decide that you actually are good enough just being who you are, as crazy and different as you are, but still good enough?"

Still, Sleator feels that the environment created by his parents had profoundly positive effects on both him and his siblings. "So much was given to us, and by that I don't just mean material things," he says. "I often wonder if I would have amounted to anything at all if my parents hadn't exposed us to so much—literature and music and science, camping trips all over the country." He continues:

> I don't know anybody who had as *interesting* a childhood as I did. Our house was a hangout for all our friends, because my parents were so relaxed, and so much fun. There were always parties. And my parents were nonconformists, and proud of it. The basic attitude was, "Why should you care what society thinks about you? Just be yourself." For instance, it never bothered my parents that Vicky sucked her thumb when she was little. And once we were in an elevator, and Vicky was sucking her thumb, and some woman in the elevator, a complete stranger, said, "You shouldn't suck your thumb, little girl." So Vicky obediently took her thumb out of her mouth. And our mother said, "Vicky, put your thumb back in your mouth!"

Vicky and Bill were always very close—she is a year and a half younger than he—and he insists he hardly ever picked on her. His two brothers are 9 and 11 years younger than Bill. He says his mother used to complain that just when he and Vicky had got old enough to be on their own, there she was taking care of infants and changing diapers again. "But she always worked when we were kids," he says, "and I'm sure that was all to the good. Even then, we somehow knew that it was better to have a mother who had her own career, rather than a mother who hovered over us constantly, as some of our friends' mothers did."

Bill's parents' nonconformist attitude during the children's formative years had a lasting effect on all of them. Sleator says:

> We all grew up to be oddballs, like they are. Actually, Danny and Tycho turned out to be more what our parents had in mind

for all of us—both of them are scientists, Danny a computer scientist, Tycho a physicist. Naturally my parents, being academics, were not thrilled when, after college, I decided not to go to graduate school, so that I could try to be a writer. They were afraid they would have to support me because I'd never make a living. Now they're proud of me. But it is still good that Danny and Tycho *did* fulfill all our parents' expectations. It took some of the pressure off.

Harvard

Following high school graduation Sleator went to Harvard. About his qualification he says, "It certainly wasn't my grades that got me in—I was eighty-fifth in a high school class of 530. I got in because I had the knack for taking those big standardized tests, the SATs and National Merit." He also told the Harvard admissions officer that he had gone to the Yale interview to get out of gym—just as he told the Yale interviewer he went to the Harvard interview to get out of gym. Harvard accepted him on early admissions. But by 15 April, the normal admissions date, Harvard had changed its mind and sent him a rejection. His mother and father were upset. They asked "some of their influential friends at Washington University to write letters to Harvard, saying it was unethical to accept someone and then reject him. And my father talked to the dean of admissions on the phone and was extremely cool about it, very logical, reasonable, unemotional." Sleator thinks it was the exceptional way his dad handled it that got him back into Harvard—"where I went on to spend the most miserable four years of my life."

He says now that going to Harvard was a great waste of his parents' money: "Harvard may be a good school for scientists and scholars, but it's not a place for artists. It spent too much time on teaching its students to analyze and interpret works of art instead of concentrating on creating them." He was miserable, but he did write several intensely tragic novellas, composed music for student films and plays, served on the editorial board of the *Crimson,* and kept a journal that contained more than 1,000 typed pages. He says he "told the journal everything, much of it drivel, but it was a cheap alternative to a psychotherapist." He gave the journal volumes individual titles, such as *Rats Live on No Evil Star.*

Even though he disliked Harvard, Sleator received his B.A. from there in 1967. He says, "I didn't drop out, as lots of people were doing in the sixties, because I hated it so much I just wanted to get it over with as quickly as possible. I started out majoring in music, but I did so badly in the theoretical courses—they never let me take a composition course, though I had been composing music for years—that the music department suggested I major in something else, and I switched to English."

The Year in England

After graduation Sleator spent a year in England (1967–68) where he studied musical composition privately and had a job as a pianist at the Royal Ballet School and the Rambert School. He says, "When I was at Harvard I earned my spending money by working as a pianist at the Cambridge School of Ballet. The technique of playing for ballet classes was probably the most important thing I learned during the four years I was in college—it has certainly proved more useful to me in my life than anything I learned at Harvard. Good ballet pianists are always in demand, and the schools in England hired me illegally—I did not have a work permit."

It was during this year in England that he had the experiences that led to his first novel, *Blackbriar.* Finding a place to live in London was difficult. Sleator didn't want to live alone, because he didn't know anybody; he wanted to find some people with an apartment who were looking for a roommate. And so for the first month or so, he moved from one student hostel to another, since a person could stay in any given hostel only for one week. Sleator would get up early every morning and wait in the line on the street to buy the newspaper with the roommate ads in it. Next, waiting in the long line at the public phone booth, he would read the ads and circle the ones that looked good. Then he would get on the phone and make appointments. So many people were

Esther Sleator pushing her children Vicky and Billy
in swing, St. Louis, 1949.

Billy and Vicky, family Christmas card, 1950.

Billy with siblings Danny, Vicky, and "Tycho," St. Louis, 1958.

A famous family photo of a tied-up Tycho (Vicky is at left), St. Louis, 1959.

Billy at Georgian Bay, Canada, 1959.

Billy and Vicky, Yosemite National Park, 1960.

Christmas carols, St. Louis, 1964: Bill at piano, Tycho behind him, Vicky in profile (center left); parents Esther and Bill with Danny are at extreme left.

Around the kitchen table, St. Louis, Christmas 1964; Billy, Tycho, Danny, and Vicky.

Billy accompanied by his father on violin, St. Louis, Christmas, 1966.

With Esther at his graduation from Harvard University, Cambridge, Massachusetts, 1967.

trying to find places to live that the people with apartments would arrange to interview seekers at 15-minute intervals: "It was like getting into college. Invariably, the people I liked rejected me, and the ones who accepted me I couldn't stand."

Sleator was getting desperate, and he had to start looking for a job. He auditioned at ballet schools. When the secretary at the Rambert School, "a very imposing woman in her fifties," asked Sleator how she could reach him, he said he would have to call her, because he had no place to live. She immediately told him she had an extra room in her apartment and perhaps he could board with her: "I told her politely that I preferred to live with people my own age—and somewhere in the back of my mind it struck me as odd that she would immediately invite me to live at her place, not really knowing anything about me at all."

When he went back to the school a few days later, to learn that it had hired him, the secretary invited him to her house for dinner. She had a beautiful two-story apartment, faded Oriental rugs, an unstrung harp, and, of great importance to Sleator, a piano—he had to have a piano for composing music. She had a wonderful big kitchen with a long wooden table, a fireplace, and strings of garlic and onions, "and she was a marvelous cook—I still remember that first meal of braised beef and an apple tart, after weeks of eating cold fish pie in the hostels. There was also a very attractive young dancer at dinner that night, was planning to rent the other available room in the apartment. It was beginning to look like not such a bad place to live after all."

That same day he had finally found some young men of his own age who had an apartment and had also chosen him. After weeks of finding nothing, he now had to make a difficult decision. His roommate at the hostel told him not to worry about it—whatever decision he made would be the wrong one. And finally he decided to stay with the secretary, because she had a piano and the other place didn't.

He soon realized that the secretary expected him to be a companion and surrogate son. Whenever he went out, she had to know what he was doing, and with whom. Sleator was more restricted there, as a college graduate, than he had been as a high school student in his parents' house—and "I was not assertive enough to do much about it," he says. She also rented a cottage by the year, in Sussex, and Sleator began to realize that going with her to this cottage was his other function in her life. She claimed that her sanity depended on going to this place every weekend and that she couldn't go there alone—it was too primitive, there was no electricity or indoor plumbing, and there was too much physical work. She had to have a man there to lug things around and chop wood and so on. It was a beautiful place, an old stone building in the middle of the woods, with no road leading to it. In the eighteenth century it had been a pesthouse where people with smallpox were isolated, and in fact was the place where Edward Jenner first did his experiments with vaccination. On the cellar door were carvings that said such things as "I, Euen, was inoculated here, 1756."

According to Sleator, "It was a great place, but at 21 I did not really want to spend every weekend of the whole year I was in England with my middle-aged landlady in the middle of the woods. Still, it was a great experience for a would-be writer." Sleator wrote letters about it, the carbons of which he saved, and, of course, put a lot of information about it in his journal. Not only did that cottage eventually become the basis for *Blackbriar,* but Sleator's struggle for independence from his landlady became the basis for Danny's struggle with Philippa.

Collaboration with Blair Lent

When Sleator returned to the United States, he continued as a ballet-school pianist but also began working with Blair Lent, a writer and illustrator of children's books. In 1969 Sleator received a fellowship to the Bread Loaf Writers Conference, and the next year he and Lent published *The Angry Moon.* The influence of this man on Sleator's life and work would be hard to overestimate; he himself says the opportunity to work with Lent had "the greatest effect on my career."

At first Sleator did many of the routine jobs, which relieved Lent to write and illustrate. But Lent also gave Sleator the opportunity to produce a picture-book manuscript. One of Lent's ed-

itors, Emilie McLeod at Atlantic/Little, Brown, had been wanting
him to do a picture book based on native American material. Lent
told Sleator that if he found a native American legend that he
liked, and if he could adapt it in a way that Emilie McLeod would
accept, he would illustrate it. "I did lots of research with original
texts at the Boston Atheneum, and found this story, and wrote
the first draft in one day. That five-page draft of *The Angry Moon*
went through dozens and dozens of revisions before Emilie gave
me a contract," Sleator says. Through that collaboration he got a
wealth of firsthand experience in the world of children's books. It
is unusual for a writer to have his or her first book illustrated by
a major artist, and *The Angry Moon* was also chosen as a Caldecott Honor Book for 1971, named an American Library Association Notable Book for the years 1940–70, and nominated for an
American Book Award.

Their next project together was to be a picture book based on
the pesthouse in England. "It was Blair's idea, not mine, to do a
book about that house," Sleator says. "But though I tried and
tried to make it a picture book, I just had too much material to
fit it into that format. And so eventually it became *Blackbriar,* a
novel, published in 1972, and Blair did wonderfully evocative
prints for the jacket and illustrations. That was when I learned
that I was much better at writing novels than picture books."

But though they did not do another picture book together, the
two collaborated on another project when Sleator wrote the musical score to accompany Lent's animated film of his own picture
book, *Why the Sun and the Moon Live in the Sky.* Because of time
limitations, authentic African instruments and musicians could
not be located for the taping of the first version, and so Sleator
decided to simulate these sounds. Blair Lent remembers: "On his
initial tape, his mother shook a broom, his father banged two
sticks, one of his brothers played the cello, while the other beat
an old pair of bongos. And Bill muffled the strings of the piano he
played to make it sound like an African thumb piano. Although
his family is musical, they had not rehearsed. The music they put
together in an evening sounded primitive and childlike. Apologiz-
ing for its many imperfections, Bill humbly presented the tape to
me. I loved it."[1]

Rehearsal Pianist

Starting in 1974, Sleator worked for nine years as rehearsal pianist for the Boston Ballet. "It was a lot more stimulating working with professional dancers than with students, and I got excited about the possibilities all over again and began expanding my repertoire, using a lot of jazz in class, people like Jelly Roll Morton and Gershwin," Sleator says. While he toured around he still found time to compose three ballets (one called *Incident at Blackbriar*) that the company performed. He says, "There is no feeling like going into a theater and watching a ballet being performed to your own music. I went to every performance and basked in it. It's a lot more immediate than the response you get from people reading your books."

Sleator enjoyed many aspects of being part of the company: "Working with other people and getting involved in all the gossip and interactions was the opposite of the isolation of being a writer, and it was very exciting." But it also brought home to him how lucky he was to be able to have the independence that writing books gave him. Dancers get the thrill of performance, the exhilaration of an immediate response from a live audience, but they are constantly told what to do, can never make an independent decision, and are yelled at constantly. Thus they have neither the time nor the opportunity to learn about anything else but dancing. As a writer, Sleator could be his own boss, could write about whatever he wanted, with nobody yelling at him or telling him what to do—"and there wasn't the stress of doing something really difficult and risky in front of an audience. Not to mention [that] as a writer, you tend to get better as you get older, and as a dancer, you inevitably get worse."

He finally left that job for several reasons. He had explored all the creative possibilities of being a rehearsal pianist and had begun to see it as a rather menial position. He says, "I got tired of being a scapegoat—very often, when someone makes a mistake, the lowly rehearsal pianist gets blamed for it." He was also making more money from his books. And he began to be bothered by what he saw going on around him. A ballet company, he explains, by its very nature has to be a dictatorship. Dancers are treated like objects. But dancers at least have a union. The nondancers on the staff—the wardrobe people, the office workers, and so on—are made to feel totally expendable. Their pay is pathetically low, but if they try to ask for a raise, or complain about something, they can be instantly replaced, because other people, thinking the theater is glamorous, are waiting to take their place for a low salary. The company uses people, Sleator feels, and then discards them, with the excuse of being a "nonprofit arts organization." The atmosphere began to depress him; he didn't want to be part of it.

But Sleator thinks he might someday write an adult novel about ballet. He has already written at least one unpublished novel about a ballet school, and he has reams of material from his ballet years. He says he "would hang out backstage and take notes about what the dancers said to each other—and since I was part of everything, they didn't watch what they said in front of me. The things they said would not go well in a young adult novel—the world of ballet is too seamy and sordid." Still, he may never write about it, for he believes there is only one plot in ballet—"Young dancer struggles and becomes a star"—and he'd rather write, "Young dancer struggles and has a miserable time and is undervalued and underpaid and never becomes a star and leaves in disgust." He doesn't believe anyone would want to read that book. He says he will probably not publish a lot of good stories, such as "the time Giselle's house tipped over and knocked a dancer out cold, the time a dancer fell into the orchestra pit, and what it is like to perform in ancient Roman amphitheaters in the rain." But in some ways Sleator protests too much, and we would not be surprised to see him write a major book with ballet as the subject.

Sleator managed somehow to write even when he was with the Boston Ballet and was spending much of his time, like Humphrey in *Fingers,* on the road and in strange hotels. In some ways the writing helped him withstand the road pressures, but at the same time the limits the pianist job placed on his available time to write were severe.

Imagination Liberated

Sleator had been writing about the people he knew and the houses he had lived in, such as the cottages in *Blackbriar* and in his second novel, *Run*. But he realized that if he were going to make a living as a writer, he would have to begin using his imagination. The first result of this new orientation was *House of Stairs*. Even with invented plot and setting, the characters were based on people he had known. He says this element gets him into trouble at times, but "most of my friends have started speaking to me again." ("GW").

Over the years Sleator's dependence on reality has steadily lessened, so that by the early eighties and the time of *The Green Futures of Tycho* (1981), he was able to let his imagination go wild. He thinks this development partly reflects his increased skill as a writer. He says:

> Writing is like other skills, in that the more you do it, the better you get at it. In a way, I was lucky that my first attempts were published, because it enabled me to begin to earn a living at it, and getting paid was a powerful motivator for writing. I'm not the kind of person who could have had a full-time job and at the same time written books and sent them out and gotten rejections for years, until finally something got published. I don't have the discipline for that. But getting published early also meant that I had already published a lot before I began to find my real voice. I think this happened with *Tycho*. I suspect that in my earlier books I was trying to fit into some kind of mold, but with *Tycho* I got liberated, and my unconscious was finally out there on the page. The book does have some slight resemblance to my own childhood, and the house is like the one I grew up in—except that everything is exaggerated, a caricature.

And he hastens to assure his readers that "time travel and an attempted alien takeover of the earth did not really happen to me."

Sleator thought *Tycho* was a funny book, and his sister's husband, who read it in manuscript form, said it was the funniest thing he had ever read. "Then," says Sleator, "it got published and the reviews said, 'Grim, spine-chilling horror.' 'Powerfully malignant atmosphere.' I hadn't yet learned how to make people laugh." That didn't happen until *Interstellar Pig,* which was recognized in the reviews as a funny book. But only recently did Sleator find out, to his disappointment, that it is mostly *adults* who think the book is funny—kids take the story very seriously. Now he tries to get some humor into all his books: "I think humor is very necessary, even in a basically suspenseful story. But it doesn't always work. As a speaker, it is easy for me to make people laugh. But on the page, it is much easier for me to be scary than to be funny. Also, some ideas just don't have a lot of humor potential. I thought *The Duplicate* was going to be funny at first. But then when I brainstormed the idea, and tried to be as realistic about it as possible, I saw that having a duplicate wouldn't be funny at all; it would be a nightmare."

Writing Methods, Values, and Motivation

Sleator now composes almost exclusively at his word processor, saying, "It eliminates the gap, so you just think something and it is on the screen. You don't even have to think about the mechanics." He says one of his favorite things in life is a morning when he can get up and know he has only to write that day. He adds:

> It is interesting how rare that is. I'm kind of spoiled. When I sit down to write, I have to know that nothing is going to interrupt me. If I know I'm going to have to stop in two hours, I can't get into the book. That's why I schedule myself to write only about four days a week. The other days are for doing errands, and taking care of correspondence, and going to the gym. On writing days I do nothing but write. I usually can write for about six hours. When I start to get sloppy, I know it's time to stop. The exception is sometimes when I'm getting to the end of an exciting chapter, or the end of the book. Then the momentum carries me along, and I can just keep going—the clock starts to go faster and faster and suddenly it's dark outside. But this is rare. Usually it's a struggle.

Though Sleator did not use outlines in writing his first few books, he usually does so now. *House of Stairs* was one of the few titles to actually come before the book itself. Typically he brainstorms for 40 pages or so before he gets to page 1, "and at last I will end up with a paragraph that has everything in it, and I'll circle it and think this is the plot. Finally I know what is going to happen and who the main characters are and what the main problem is. But inevitably I will deviate from this scenario when I get into a book. When I'm right there in the middle of it, I always come up with better ideas."

An important value for Sleator is empathy, "trying to think about people different from yourself and to understand how they feel." It is acceptable to be different or even weird, not to fit into social expectations. He tells how his parents helped him with this value: "My parents were so great in that respect, of not making me fit into a mold. My mother would always say to me that girls like athletic boys now, but once you get to high school, they start respecting you for your intelligence. So, it's OK. You're fine. Don't worry. I grew up with this thing of it's OK to be different, to be whoever you are. . . . When I set out to write a story I think about the characters in terms of people who don't fit into the stereotypes . . . not making it like a TV show, not making it like a boy has to be macho or that the girl has to be feminine."

When he talks about empathy, he's saying one should be good to other people not only because it's good for them, but also because its practical. The characters in Sleator's books who have empathy are always more successful in the end, and he believes that is also true of life. Understanding *why* people do the things they do helps us get along better with them. Sleator believes that by letting people know they have done something that pleases one, they will be more likely to do it again. He adds, "It's a simple and effective behavioral strategy, and I'm constantly amazed at how rarely people use it. The ballet company was a perfect example. When a dancer gave a great performance, the director would be afraid he'd get a swelled head, and come down on him harder—it was like punishing someone for doing well, and it's backwards thinking. If you *reward* someone for doing well, he'll work harder to repeat it."

Sleator writes only one book at a time. When he starts a new book he says, "Please, God, I hope this is going to work, that it won't fall apart." His characters don't take over, as some other writers say theirs do. He has to work, to agonize over them. He obviously relies very little on inspiration. Only half-jokingly he says, "People ask me if I get writer's block, and my answer is, It depends on how much money I have in the bank. When I have a lot of money, I get writer's block. When I'm broke, then I am truly inspired. Then I can write. When the money starts to pile up, I try to get rid of it. I'll go to Asia or do something else." Right now Sleator is spending almost all his money on a complete renovation of his house—a new kitchen, bathroom, everything. He can feel the pressure of his bank account disappearing, and his new book is going better and better. He thinks it is important to be honest to kids about what creativity is—to give them the idea that being creative isn't some type of magical thing at all: "It is work, it's a job, and like any kind of job, if you expect to get paid you have to do it whether you feel like it or not. You can't depend on inspiration."

He tells this to students at schools, and he also talks to them about money, exactly how—and how much—a writer gets paid. Not many writers do so, and sometimes adults are uncomfortable with it. Sleator recently spoke at a private school, "and they actually wrote me a letter afterwards objecting to the fact that I had talked to the kids about money. It's always the most affluent places that are afraid of exposing the kids to the subject of money—the same people who try to get me to lower my fee."

Working with Editors

Sleator collaborates closely with his editors. Ann Durell at E. P. Dutton has worked with him on all but two of his books. He likes working with Ann because she is not afraid to tell him what is wrong with his manuscript and how he can improve it:

But I think I'm unusual in that respect. I feel that a lot of authors don't like an editor to tell them. People always say, "But it is your work. How can you let somebody else try to push you into doing this to it?" My answer is, If it is somebody that I trust, like Ann, then she is improving it. You need another point of view. You have to have it. I am writing about a character that I have in my mind. Usually I base my characters on people I know. The reader does not know that person. It would be very easy for me to leave out certain important things. That is why you need an editor. Ann Durell is always great: "This person wouldn't do that, or if he did do that, why?" Or "I don't understand that." Ann solidifies character and plot. She makes it come across. Occasionally I don't agree with what she says and we fight. Not really fight—*discuss*. And in the end, if I stick to my guns and come up with good reasons for why I want it my way, she will back down.

One exception was the book *Fingers*. Sleator wrote it in the summer of 1980, when the Boston Ballet company went on a three-month tour around the world—it was the first American dance company to perform in the People's Republic of China. Only four nondancers went on that trip. At that time, the budget did not allow the organization to take a pianist along. Instead the company brought tapes Sleator had made, for which he was paid $25 each. But the dance company did need someone to wash out the tights, and so a friend of his in the wardrobe department got to go on the tour. His friend had been working for the company for only six months, whereas Sleator had been with them for six years. Emotionally he felt a lot of resentment, even though logically he knew the choice made complete sense. In real life there was no appropriate way for him to express his anger.

"So," he says, "I sat down and wrote *Fingers*. And all my resentment poured out into that book. That's one of the best things about being a writer—it's a great psychological release." He didn't have to be nasty to anybody in real life; he just punished his characters. "And that's why Ann hated the book," he says. "She rejected it. She said that reading it was an unpleasant experience. And she told me not to bother sending her a revision. Nothing I could do to the book would make her change her mind about it." But she also said Sleator could try to sell it to someone else.

He sent the manuscript to Harper and Row, Macmillan, and Farrar, Straus, and they all rejected it. The problem wasn't just the bitter voice of the narrator. It was the fact that the parents were the villains; Sleator thinks that scared the editors. But it had to be that way. The book is about a child prodigy, and when Sleator did research he found that many child prodigies hated their parents. It made sense: these parents had forced the kids to practice eight hours a day, starting at age two, and then made them give concerts and kept all the money. They took away their childhoods. The book was realistic in that sense, but it still alienated the editors—until Sleator sent it to Jean Karl at Atheneum. He comments, "She thought the book was funny, as I did, and she bought it. By that time I had done so much work on it that it needed only one more revision. Stylistically, I think it is my best written book. I don't know why it came out that way, but it did. And I've tried to get back to that particular style in other books, and somehow I just can't."

Travels in Thailand

The Duplicate is another example of Sleator's state of mind being channeled into the book he was writing. In the summer of 1986 his very good friends, the writer Raboo Rodgers and his wife, Beck, were renting a house in Bangkok for several months and invited him to visit them. "I didn't want to go," Sleator says. "I had never been to Asia; I knew nothing about Thailand. But I also felt it was an opportunity I couldn't refuse, to visit these good friends who were living in Asia, and I had plenty of money. So I went for only 17 days."

It was an experience that changed his life. He'd never been to a place he liked so much; he felt more at home in Bangkok than he had in London. He says it is hard to explain the appeal of it, since he saw Bangkok as an ugly city: "Most of the old buildings were wooden, and have fallen down, replaced by cheap, nondescript concrete structures, and most of the canals have been paved over. Not to mention it's hot, humid, polluted, and the traffic is abominable." But he loved it because of the people. The Thai people are friendly and know how to have fun: "Almost any situation is an excuse for a party, for celebration," Sleator says. The

Thais are unusual in that they actually *like* Americans. Thailand is the only country in Southeast Asia that was never a colonial possession of a Western power, and so Westerners mean not oppression but money and glamor.

Sleator's friends took him on a trip to Chieng Rai, in the North. They traveled partly by train—and the trains were old-fashioned, were civilized, and had wonderful food. They also traveled by riverboat, despite the risk of bandits. The boat broke down halfway through the trip, and they were stranded in a village for hours and enjoyed every minute of it.

When they finally landed outside Chieng Rai, they hired bicycle rickshas to take them to town; then their guide, Kob, rented a minibus to take them to his parents' house. The parents are rice farmers. Kob refused to phone them; he said it should be a surprise, that they would be delighted to have guests arrive at eight in the evening with no warning. Recalls Sleator: "And they were. We sat down on the floor; they brought out a mat; we brought out our whiskey, and Kob cooked a delicious meal—while his family sat clustered together watching us from the other end of the room. We stayed there for several days, traveling with them to the Burmese border, and they gradually became more comfortable with us. They were poor, but very generous. They wouldn't let us repay them for their hospitality until finally we bribed the minibus driver to stop at a restaurant so we could take them all out to dinner." The restaurant was only a kilometer from their house, but they had never eaten there, because they could not afford it. They all sat at a long table, and when Sleator looked up, he noticed there were hundreds of lizards crawling around on the ceiling.

When the 17 days were over, Sleator came back to the United States, wanting only to return to Thailand. But he had too many obligations. The first thing he did was to write down everything that had happened on the trip. At Raboo's suggestion, he had recorded it all on a pocket tape recorder while it was happening, and in one week he had turned the tape into a 138-page memoir—some of which he hopes to incorporate into his next book. Meanwhile he was broke and had to come up with something he could sell, and so he wrote *The Duplicate,* about a young man who makes a copy of himself, thinking that the duplicate will fulfill all his obligations so that he can be free to do whatever he wants. Sleator says he had no idea he was writing about his own state of mind until six months after the book was published. Then he looked at the book, and all at once he saw that the central emotion in it was his yearning to go back to Thailand: "It's unconscious, it's not there in a concrete way, but nevertheless that state of mind is what gives the book any emotional validity it may have. . . . Probably all my books have a direct if unconscious connection to what was going on in my life when I wrote them."

Sleator has been back to Thailand twice since his first trip. The following summer he spoke at the International Reading Association conference in Bangkok. There he met educators who asked him to speak to their classes, and those contacts led to another trip in December 1988. He says he would still like to live there someday.

The Boston House and Other Pastimes

Sleator is currently very involved with remodeling the Victorian row house in Boston that he and some friends own. He says it gives him plenty of things to do when he is not writing. He also spends time traveling, speaking at schools and conferences, "exercising fanatically," and, for a while, cooking: "I got obsessed with French puff pastry. It's like sculpture. At one time I thought that cooking would be a good way to make ends meet between royalty checks, which come only two times a year. I professionally catered several big parties. That's how I found out that catering was not a great way to make money—it's too grueling and stressful, and too much work for the money you get. Writing *Singularity* was more fun, and even, in a certain way, *easier* than doing a buffet dinner for 70. Lecturing is a much better way to make extra money." He considers himself fortunate to be a writer and does not believe he will ever run out of ideas, since the world is filled "with great things like quasars and tachyons and the Mandelbrot set."

2. Works for Children: Sleator Novels in Miniature

The Angry Moon

William Sleator's entry into the world of professional writing came, as we have seen, by way of children's literature, through Sleator's serving as assistant to a well-known illustrator. Through this relationship Sleator came to retell a Tlingit Indian story, and that story became the text for a Caldecott Honor Book, *The Angry Moon* (1970). Illustrated by Blair Lent, the book is a somewhat-frightening, but at the same time delightful, book for children ages five to eight.

Lupan and Lapowinsa have been together constantly on earth all their lives, until the angry moon separates them by engulfing Lapowinsa in a rainbow and abducting her from earth to punish her for laughing at the funny marks on his face. To rescue her, Lupan leaves the earth by climbing to the sky country on a chain made by the arrows he has shot into the sky. Lupan seems to change from a boy to a man as the story unfolds. He must go through dangerous feats to get to Lapowinsa. He meets a grandmother who prepares him for the final task of saving his friend. She feeds him, to give him back his strength after the long journey, and gives him a pinecone, a fish eye, a rose, and a small stone to help him in battle against the moon.

Lupan finds Lapowinsa sticking out of the smoke hole of the house of the moon, being scorched by the fire. He rescues her and puts the pinecone in her place. As in most of Sleator's stories, there is a nightmarish quality here. The angry moon is huge, a mask of tumbling evil, as it chases the children through the sky. The moon rolls after them faster than they can run. Lupan throws the fish eye behind him, and where it falls a large lake appears. Because the moon is going so fast and cannot stop in time, he slides into the water. By the time the moon gets out and rolls around the lake, he is far behind. He almost catches up with them again. Lupan tosses the rose behind him, and a rose thicket rises and entangles the moon. On getting untangled, he rolls even faster. Lupan tosses the stone—a gigantic mountain that the moon cannot climb appears. He rolls helplessly up and down. Lupan and Lapowinsa descend to safety on the ladder of arrows. When they do return to the village, everyone is glad to see them and wants to hear their story, which is later handed down from generation to generation.

The story is mostly told through narration, with some dialogue. The language is basic and simple, the style is loose and easy, but the book does not have much humor. Even though in most of Sleator's later works a weak male character will be featured (always becoming stronger through someone else's need), Lupan is strong from the beginning. His loyalty to his friend makes him become stronger; however, he is dependent on the grandmother who gives him the magical articles to held him find Lapowinsa. The grandmother is portrayed as good, the opposite of the moon. She is kind and loving but does not interfere with Lupan's pursuit of Lapowinsa—a portent of future adults in Sleator's works.

Reviewer Ethna Sheehan writes, "*The Angry Moon* is a story full of atmosphere, and Blair Lent's Tlingit-inspired illustrations in somber moonlit and sunlit hues orchestrate the drama of this tale."[1] And Elizabeth Minot Graves calls it "the most stunning and original picture book of the season. Vibrant, imaginative paintings and a spare and thrilling text."[2]

Sleator himself says this about *The Angry Moon*:

I don't remember much about working on this book, it was so long ago. As it says on the copyright page, the story is a Tlingit Indian legend, recorded by Dr. John R. Swanton in the *Bulletin of the Bureau of American Ethnology*. I found the story in the Boston Athenaeum, an old private library. I wrote the first draft of my picture-book adaptation in one day. I then worked on it for months and months with Emilie McLeod, a perfectionist, who correctly felt that in a picture book, which has so few words, every word has to be exactly right. It's like writing a poem. It was a great experience for me to have such a careful and hardworking editor on my first book.

Among the Dolls

Although *Among the Dolls* (1975) is placed here in the section on children's books, it was actually written after *House of Stairs* (1974), surely one of Sleator's finest works. Ann Durell suggested he change pace "completely with a fantasy about a girl and a doll-house." As Durell remembers it, she suggested a story for 9- to 11-year-olds because librarians had been telling her there was a need for science fiction and fantasy for this age-group. She concludes, "And what a story—his device of a doll-house-within-a-dollhouse still impresses me." Sleator says of Durell's contributions, "I suspect it was probably Ann's idea that the one doll who helps Vicky should be a new one, not originally from the doll-house, that Vicky buys herself. That's the kind of logical and effective device that Ann always comes up with."

Among the Dolls has illustrations by Trina Schart Hyman that Sleator calls "perfect," with the dolls looking "exactly the way I had imagined them, and that happens very rarely." The book is about Vicky (named for Sleator's sister), who wishes for a 10-speed bicycle for her birthday. She drops hints about her wish, including the color and style of her desired bicycle. When Vicky's birthday arrives, much to her surprise she unwraps not a shiny brand-new 10-speed bicycle but a brown and dusty antique doll-house. The dolls look used, disfigured, and chipped. Vicky is so disappointed that she rejects the dollhouse, her birthday, and her parents, and runs upstairs crying. Her birthday is ruined. Vicky's parents can't understand her outrage at what they thought was the perfect gift.

While Vicky is up in her bedroom pouting and ignoring her mother and father, they are arguing and ignoring each other. When Vicky begins to play with the dollhouse, she is cruel to the dolls in many ways. She characterizes the mother doll as nasty, overpowering, and mean to her family, especially her husband. The mother doll makes her husband sleep on the hard lumpy sofa, and instead of showing love for him she yells and screams and calls him insulting names. As Vicky cruelly manipulates the dolls, including a new plastic baby doll she buys, her own happy family falls apart. Just as she makes the mother and father dolls quarrel, so do her own parents argue. Freak accidents happen almost daily. Suddenly one day Vicky finds herself inside the dollhouse, at the mercy of the dolls she has tormented.

Vicky has a fight for survival, since her reduced size takes away her advantage over the dolls. She fears for her life and needs help with an escape. Jumping out of the dollhouse will not work. Her only hope is Dandaroo, the new doll. He explains to her that she has to get into the attic and find the miniature replica of her own house; the bizarre happenings are being caused by the manipulation of her family by the grudge-holding dolls, and Vicky has to enter the replica in the attic in order to get out of the hell she has created. With only seconds to spare, she escapes back to the safety of her room. Days later the dollhouse is given to a neighbor, and Vicky and her parents become the same loving family that existed before the gift. The only remnant Vicky keeps from the dollhouse is the cheap plastic doll that saved her life.

Sleator's portrayal of neglect is effective. In the beginning Vicky is shy and has no friends. She wants to get out more and expand her universe and she sees a bike as a way to do that. Instead she gets a musty old dollhouse that causes her to contract rather than expand, to go more inside herself until finally she becomes a doll trapped inside the dollhouse and sees all the fighting, neglect, and hate that she has partly caused. When she escapes the dollhouse at last and rejoins the larger world, she looks worn-out and pale. Her parents then decide she has been spending too much time inside with the dolls and the dollhouse. They suggest she needs to be out more and to make some new friends.

In the beginning the book has a lighthearted, cheery tone, employing such words as *shimmered, dreamily, carefree,* and *beautiful.* The tone gradually becomes gloomy as words like *miserable, dispiritedly,* and *helpless* are used. Sleator says he remembers almost nothing about writing the book, but he knows the idea came from the way his sister, Vicky, used to make the inhabitants of her dollhouse fight with one another: "I'm sure it was a healthy psychological release for her, and I'm sure many children unleash hostilities onto their dolls. But I had never come across a book that described what dolls might naturally feel about being treated this way, if they were conscious. In the dollhouse books I'd seen, the dolls always loved the kid who pushed them around, whereas I would have expected them to resent it. And so I came up with this story."

Booklist calls it "a fast-paced, chilling fantasy of three telescoped worlds that affect each other in a vicious cycle." The reviewer concludes that the suspense is clutching, the dolls real, the implications scary.[3] The book is reminiscent of such works as *The Doll's House,* by Rumer Godden, one of Sleator's favorite authors. In *The Doll's House* Godden says that it is a dangerous thing to be a doll because dolls cannot choose but can only be chosen, and that they can't do but can only be done to. Sleator clearly shows his skill here in articulating children's fears—a skill to be used even more effectively in later works.

Once, Said Darlene

William Sleator's works have been illustrated by some of the best and most successful book artists of the day—Blair Lent, Trina Shart Hyman, and, for *Once, Said Darlene* (1979), Steven Kellogg. Like other female characters in Sleator's works, Darlene is strong and in control. It is hard to tell whether the stories she tells are just made up or are about magic that really happened. In all her adventures Darlene leaves behind some object, such as a white umbrella, a pair of white gloves, or a white telescope. None of her friends believe her stories, except perhaps Peter (the same name as the protagonist in *House of Stairs*), who does not know whether they are true or not. As Darlene's tales get more and more elaborate, her listeners ridicule her—until at last Peter says he believes. Suddenly he and Darlene are transported to the world she has been describing in her stories; she really had been banished by an evil magician. Thus, as in *Peter Pan* the world of the imagination is something one can enter only if one believes. But here a person can enter and leave at will. Darlene tells Peter he can go home whenever he wants.

The humorous, somewhat-childlike illustrations by Kellogg add much to this story. The drawings of children in the real world are just as realistic as the imaginative illustrations of the fantasy world are fanciful. The book ends with Darlene and Peter riding on a unicorn up into the sky. Sleator's characters are going to enter and leave such worlds over and over again—through magic, outer-space dimensions, dreams, ESP, time travel, black holes, duplications, reversing, board games, and strange attractors.

As to how this book evolved, Sleator says he had always wanted to write a book about a compulsive liar. He had a friend in high school who was always talking about her impressive accomplishments and telling stories about her many wild and exciting experiences. Eventually Bill and some of her other friends began comparing notes, and it became apparent that this girl was inventing a great deal of what she said about herself. As is often the case, he connects the origin of this book with the need for cash: "Broke again, I began looking for an idea for a picture book. I figured that a picture book, with a manuscript of only five pages, might generate an advance a lot faster than a novel. And I thought, what if there was a kid who was always talking about her extravagant exploits, and soon everybody believed she was a compulsive liar—and then it turned out that everything she said was true. A simple concept with a real surprise ending, and the best picture book idea I've ever had. (My mother considers this my best book.)"

He wrote the first draft as a traditional picture book. Ann Durell liked the idea but thought it would work better as an easy-to-read book, written at first-grade level. Her suggestions: Keep the sentences and the paragraphs short. Limit the vocabulary as much as possible—and if it's necessary to use a long word, go for one that follows simple phonetic rules, and use the word several times so that the child can learn to recognize it. It was also Durell's idea to organize the book in short chapters, each one following the same narrative pattern, and to repeat certain phrases, such as "Once, said Darlene."

Sleator assesses the results of his efforts:

> I have to admit that it was a struggle to write something within these limitations that did not sound sappy. And I wasn't 100 percent successful. It is a major flaw in this book that all the objects Darlene talks about are white—if only I'd picked some other color to keep repeating!
>
> Of course, the illustrations by Steven Kellogg are a big part of the appeal of this book. I wish it was still in print.

Ann Durell was pleased with the book. She says it "has always seemed to me to be an extremely satisfying first-grade story, stronger in characterization and psychological meaning than most such books, yet at a comfortable reading level. It is really a Sleator novel in miniature."

That's Silly

Ann Durell characterizes *That's Silly* (1981) with the same words: "a William Sleator novel in miniature." In this book, illustrated by Laurence Di Fiori, two playmates, Tom and Rachel, have unusual experiences with reality, pretending, and magic.

The playmates are not always sure which is which. The book begins with the two swinging and Tom calling it flying; Rachel says they are merely swinging. According to Tom, the lemonade they drink is magic; to Rachel it's just lemonade. Pretending is silly to Rachel.

Rachel finds a small doll's head that Tom thinks may be magic. When Rachel makes a wish while holding the doll's head, the wishes seem to come true. Tom and Rachel experience various adventures, including going inside a picture she has drawn and taking a balloon ride. Rachel loses the doll's head but finds a doll's hand that may or may not have the same kind of magic in it. To Tom's "Do you think it's magic?" Rachel answers, "I do not know, but I can find out."

Sleator says of *That's Silly,* "This book is an example of an idea, unlike *Once, Said Darlene,* which is a little too complex to work in a picture-book format. It probably would have worked better in a format like *Among the Dolls.* But I do like the idea of a kid getting stuck in her own primitive drawing."

This story of Tom and Rachel's magic could go on forever, and so it is with almost every book Bill Sleator writes, whether it's the singularity of the shed in *Singularity,* the pig in *Interstellar Pig,* the Spee-Dee-Dupe in *The Duplicate,* or the phaser in *Strange Attractors.* Sleator always has an instrument or a gimmick for allowing us to slip away from the "surly bonds of earth." He also finds a way to strike a balance and avoid complete chaos.

3. Young Adult Mysteries: Place and Plot Predominate

It could be that Sleator turned to young adult literature, specifically the novel, because he found picture books so hard to write. In his book of interviews with modern young adult authors, *Behind the Covers,* Jim Roginski asked Sleator what form he found particularly difficult. Sleator answered:

> Probably a picture book. A picture book is a five-page manuscript that goes through a lot of revisions. It is different from a novel. There are so many fewer words. It's almost more like a poem. Every word you have needs to be exactly right because there are so few. You have to have an idea that's so clear and so right in every way, and is so simple and so elegant. Everything has to fit together. It's like a puzzle.
>
> I feel I express myself better in a novel format. (Roginski, 199)

And so he moved on into young adult literature and his first novel, *Blackbriar* (1972). It was Blair Lent who suggested he write about the pesthouse he'd known in England. Sleator says Lent had some "wonderful and spooky ideas for a picture book, but I couldn't shape it into a picture-book format—I just had too much material." Emilie McLeod suggested he might try it as a young adult novel. Sleator spent about a year on the first draft, finally sending it off to her. She didn't like it, and he was very disappointed; however, she did suggest he get the opinion of another editor.

Ann Durell says the manuscript for the book came to her from Blair Lent, with whom she had worked on several books, including the Caldecott winner *The Funny Little Woman,* by Arlene Mosel. Durell read the manuscript with interest but had some serious reservations about it. Among them: "It was a Gothic tale set in England, and Bill was at a disadvantage since such stories depend heavily on atmosphere. As an American, he lacked that deeply ingrained sense of cultural nuances that are so important to a true evocation of place, especially the elements of the past, which form an integral part of a gothic plot like this."

But she was caught up by the work's unusual quality. She was impressed that Danny, the main character, and Philippa, his guardian, were more than stock characters. She was also pleased that the narrative viewpoint was not hackneyed.

Durell describes the beginning of the successful author-editor relationship between Slater and her as follows: "After I read the manuscript, I met and talked to Bill, and I not only liked him, but most important, found him remarkably easy to communicate with. And as I've said, rapport between editor and author is crucial to the success of the relationship, especially on a book that would require as much revision as this one. So I wanted to work with him. And he did do a great deal of revision on *Blackbriar,* making it into a book I was pleased to publish."

The book, based on the journal Sleator had kept in England, is in many ways about the house he lived in, one of a series of houses that were to become the basis of books. He says, "I think it was the fact that I was describing real experiences that made my first stumbling effort as successful as it was. That plus the tremendous amount of help I received from my editor, Ann Durell." This appreciation continues through all of the books she has edited for him.

Blackbriar is about a boy who becomes an adult through learning more about himself and responsibility. The setting is rural England, mainly at an estate known as Blackbriar, with surrounding hills and ridges, and nearby an ancient burial ground of Druid kings. Fifteen-year-old Danny Chilton lives with Philippa, the widowed secretary at his school. His father and mother are dead, and his legal guardian, Mr. Bexford, has actually seen Danny only once, although he does send the annual check from the annuity the boy's mother had left him. Before Philippa took Danny to live at Blackbriar he was afraid and insecure, and would go into dreamy trances. When Philippa and Danny arrive in Dunchester and ask about Blackbriar, people look at them suspiciously and become silent. Although their reactions frighten Philippa, Danny is excited at the possibility that their country house may not be so dull after all.

Danny soon makes friends with Lark Hovington, a young girl with whom he explores the house and its surroundings, including the burial grounds. Danny meets Lark for the first time on a visit to the Tumuli mounds, said to be the burial grounds for three Druid kings. He is able to talk to her in a way he has not been able to talk to anyone else before. Through Lark, Danny discovers that his need to become independent does not mean he needs to become independent of everyone. An attraction develops between the two.

They talk about the strangeness of Blackbriar, which has been unoccupied (at least by human beings) for as long as anyone can remember. The local folk prefer it that way, for they know the house was once used as a pesthouse during the great plague of the seventeenth century. Blackbriar houses secrets and some things not so secret, such as a door leading to the basement with names carved into it, among them Mary Peachy. All the names except hers have the date of death beneath. In the basement Danny finds a passage leading underground. He and Lark explore it and find that it contains many skeletons and ends at a stairway under the mansion of Lord Harleigh, a neighbor.

Danny has had a dream about fires since moving to Blackbriar. He tells Lark about it: A strange procession was winding across barren hillsides by moonlight. People in black robes chanted solemnly, monotonously, holding blazing torches above their heads. At the front of the procession were three crowned men dressed in white. The procession dragged on and on over the same hills with the droning heavy chanting always underneath. He couldn't tell whether he was in the procession or whether he was only watching it. But all the time he knew that something else was there, huge and dark and menacing, lurking just beyond the torchlight, waiting and watching. Immediately after waking, he hears the distant laughter of a woman. Lark has seen and heard actual happenings that tend to corroborate Danny's dream—fires burning up on the burial mounds, with crowds of people singing. This dream, along with what Lark has actually seen, seems to be pulling Danny on, and he develops independence as he and Lark puzzle through the bizarre events.

Philippa seems to have an need to manage Danny's life. She insists that he go to the town library and keep up with studies that are more important to her than to him. She is hovering and possessive to the extent that she tries to keep him from forming any friendships, particularly with girls. Philippa quickly becomes jealous of Lark.

After several mysterious happenings, Philippa and her Siamese cat, Islington, disappear. Danny and Lark, using the secret passage, find her locked up in Lord Harleigh's mansion. They send her to Lark's father while they search for Islington. They also discover a picture of Mary Peachy holding a doll, with an inscription under the picture revealing that she was tried as a witch in 1665, convicted, and sentenced to Blackbriar. She died there, but not of the plague. Danny recognizes the wooden doll in the picture as the doll Islington found earlier at Blackbriar. From the moment of its discovery, both Islington and Philippa are repelled by the doll. Danny was supposed to have thrown it away, but he still has it with him. Perhaps some power is guiding him? Maybe it is Mary? Maybe she is a witch? The young people go to the burial mounds, where they find Satan worshipers just at the point of sacrificing Islington. The high priest says he has drawn Belial, one of the most powerful fiends of hell, into the body of the cat. The high priest turns out to be Lord Harleigh. Danny protects himself with the wooden doll, which seems to possess great importance for Lord Harleigh. Islington is flung into the fire, but Danny rescues him and throws the doll into the fire instead. The

entire congregation turns on Danny, but just in time the local police, accompanied by Philippa and Lark's father, arrive.

The police are amazed by Danny's bravery—he has dealt successfully with something the entire community has been ignoring
for years. The citizens of Dunchester have believed in witchcraft
all these years, or at least have been duped into standing around
on hillsides and dancing, chanting, and coming close to killing
two young people and a cat. The police dismiss the townspeople,
telling them to go home and behave themselves.

At the conclusion Mr. Bexford takes Danny back to London to
attend a boarding school. Philippa opens a restaurant in Dunchester, where Danny occasionally visits her. But when they walk
around Blackbriar they do not enter the house: "Danny could not
forget the sound of Mary Peachy's voice . . . the house that would
always belong to her alone."

Danny's struggle for independence is one of the main themes of
the novel. He is growing up and wants to take greater responsibility for his own life. As he begins to take charge of his life, Philippa tries to maintain her control of him, but then faces the
inevitable, and their roles are reversed as she becomes almost too
dependent on him. According to Margaret Daggett in her *English
Journal* article, "Growing up and mastering the world is a basic
appeal of young adult books, but the supernatural adventure
story allows readers to identify with a protagonist who's gone one
step further. This hero has seen through the facade of adult worries and goals. This hero reaches for a greater understanding of
life and power over life."[1]

When Ann Durell read the original manuscript she felt the
characters of Danny and Philippa were inconsistent and vague.
Sleator says in his mind he knew exactly who these characters
were—himself and his landlady. But the characters had to work
for the reader, and real incidents had to be changed to make that
happen. Sleator learned a great deal about characterization
through working on it in *Blackbriar* with Durell's help, but, he
says, "This is not to say I mastered characterization. I think it is
still my weakest point as a writer."

Ann Durell also suggested a change in the original name of the neighbor—Lord Gravesend—which Sleator changed to Lord Harleigh. She suggested the mansion be made more realistic. In the original version a large circular staircase went up and up for many flights. Sleator says it was "very surreal." (Perhaps that was recycled in *House of Stairs?*) He also had the cat, Islington, burning to death. He says, "I had hated my landlady's cat in England, and got a lot of satisfaction out of killing him in this book. But Ann is a great lover of Siamese cats and did not want the cat to die. And in fact, having the protagonist—who also hates the cat—save him in the end was a much more satisfying conclusion in terms of character."

Sleator can make the unreal seem real; he can help readers suspend their disbelief. His power to do so without becoming too detailed, descriptive, or technical, and to move readers along as if they were imagining and creating the story themselves, is an ability that developed even more fully in later novels. Of course, he does not achieve this aspect completely in his first work for young adults, his first mystery. As the *Publishers Weekly* reviewer wrote of the paperback edition, "Neither the characterization nor the plot is entirely convincing, but as a whole, it offers a couple of hours of suspenseful entertainment." Not bad, since entertainment was surely what Sleator was primarily after anyway.

A *Library Journal* reviewer, less kind, stated that despite Sleator's efforts, *Blackbriar* "is essentially an implausible story" that is "so contrived that the story remains totally unconvincing." Almost surely Sleator was not even attempting to create a realistic story. The *Publishers Weekly* reviewer is more on the mark: "*Blackbriar* is a place where an adolescent, even an adult, can escape to and still get something realistic and lasting about humans and how they behave. Maybe even something about how and why they grow."[4]

Run

Sleator's second novel in his pre–science fiction period was again based on an actual house he had lived in, and in the beginning, like *Blackbriar,* it was a collaborative storytelling with his friend Blair Lent. One spring they were both working in a house on the ocean—or at least Lent was working, finishing his latest picture book. Sleator was searching for an idea. The idea came, as he tells it at the end of the book, from a herring run behind their house. Gulls were out in noisy swarms to catch the herring, which were trying to swim to safety. He and Lent, during a walk on the beach, began to compose a complicated story about the place. One idea began to take over—"the struggle between the gulls and the fish would have its counterpart in the human events of the story." By the end of their walk they had worked out the plot of *Run* (1973).

Perhaps they should have walked longer. The parallel of the "run" of the fish and the "run" of the people is not entirely clear. The fish are running for survival; the people (except the drug addict, a minor character) have no particular reason to be running and aren't really running at all.

From the very beginning of *Run* Sleator deliberately, perhaps too deliberately, attempts to establish a mysterious, eerie atmosphere. In a one-page preface titled "Fear," two boys on bikes are stranded by the tide. Gulls wheel and dart above their heads, almost hitting them. Soon the rain begins and muffles their cries. One of the boys manages to lean the bikes against the back wall of a nearby house: "Then, as he turned to go inside, he saw a moving shape among the trees. Not a sea gull, something bigger, more like a large animal or even a person. Vague and indistinct, he thought that this *must* be an illusion of the rain, for it vanished quickly. But suddenly he was chilled. Shivering, he hurried into the room." This "Fear" section is to be completely repeated later in the book in its true context and is apparently here as a kind of teaser, a hook, a mood-and-atmosphere setter. Its actual function is to confuse both time and point of view.

At the opening of chapter 1, 15-year-old Lillian is at home by herself because her parents have gone visiting for the weekend. Standing outside on the shore looking at the house, she notices how empty, isolated, and foreboding it looks. She wants to prove she is mature enough to stay alone, but she is not really so sure about it herself. She notices the two boys who have been stranded on what was the beach by the incoming tide. She takes a boat out and rescues the two, Jerry and Mark, and convinces them to come into her house.

They find the door open, and suddenly Lillian is afraid; it had been closed when she went down to the beach. A hard rain begins to fall, and soon the young people are caught up in preparing lunch and getting to know one another. Mark is a serious young man, and although at first Lillian doesn't like his attitude, toward the end of the book she understands and appreciates his personality. Jerry is cheerful and outgoing. They soon discover the radio is missing. While they hunt for it their lunch burns to a crisp. Thinking about the open door and the missing radio and afraid of being alone, Lillian tries to get the boys to stay as long as possible. They play three games of Clue, and by then it is too dark and stormy for the boys to continue their bike trip. Lillian convinces them to stay for dinner, a meal she and Jerry prepare very messily. At dinner Lillian serves wine, which she has never drunk before. Dinner is a parent's nightmare as the three spill wine on the rug, leave ice cream out on the kitchen counter to melt, and pass out at the table.

Mark awakens to the screams of sea gulls and goes out to rescue the bikes from the tide. When the others wake up to the mess they have made, Mark tells them about the sea gulls. Lillian explains there are so many of them because of the spawning run of the herring up the stream nearby.

Lillian's parents call to say they are staying in the city another night. She asks to stay with a neighbor for the night, rather than joining them in the city. But when she tries to call the neighbor she finds that the phone has been disconnected; hence she will be on her own for one more night.

The teenagers decide to go up the stream to see how many herring get through to their spawning grounds. Lillian is sickened not only by the gulls killing the fish but also by the townspeople, who are out catching bucketfuls of them. When the teenagers return to the house the TV is gone. Lillian goes out to get wood and discovers someone is hiding behind the woodpile. She attempts to call the police, but Mark rips the phone out of the wall. Frightened, Lillian seeks refuge in bed, only to awaken as a strange man comes into the room and sits by her bed. Lillian babbles on about herself, the day's adventures, and why she screamed when she saw him earlier, until finally she runs out of things to say. The intruder apologizes for scaring her and leaves. As she tells Jerry and Mark what has just happened, the police arrive. They are warning the whole community to watch out for weirdos—no doubt drug addicts—who have robbed several houses in the area. Suspicious of Lillian's being alone with two young men, the police question the three about drugs and finally go on their way. Strangely enough, Lillian doesn't breathe a word about the intruder. When the three later surprise the man as he tries to steal her father's electric saw, he confesses he is a drug addict. He explains his unfortunate problem, and the trio feels pity for him and wants to help and protect him.

This redemption theme is hard to believe, but the man is an outcast, seen by the teenagers to be lonely, hunted, and helpless. He is so addicted that he looks totally wretched and dissipated and, of course, shakes uncontrollably. Despite his wealthy family, his addiction is so advanced that they can't do anything for him, since he refuses to be put into a clinic or other type of institution. He says he knows through experience that such a step won't help. Stealing and selling items for drugs are all that are left for him for the rest of his life—which turns out to be not long: the police arrive, the three advise the man to run, but he is shot down while trying to escape. Lillian is left to clean up the mess and to face her parents on their return.

Originally the intruder was supposed to be a Vietnam War veteran who became a heroin addict while taking part in research. Sleator says, "I read books by people who had been in Vietnam. But Ann felt that making him a Vietnam veteran was a bit too much, that it made the book seem like a social tract, so we dropped the part about him being in Vietnam and just made him a junkie."

The incident in the bedroom was based on a real happening; the animator of *Why the Sun and the Moon Live in the Sky* had told Sleator and Blair Lent about an experience she once had while staying in the country. Says Sleator, "In the middle of the night a man wearing a mask had walked into her bedroom, sat down, and just stared at her, not saying a word. She didn't know what to do, and was terrified, and her response was just to keep talking. She talked and talked, and finally the guy just got up and silently left. And this became an important scene in the book."

Though the drug addict appears to be a crazy wretch, a mysterious monster, he turns out to be merely a desperate, lonely human being, and not a very interesting one. Probably many readers find this aspect disappointing.

All three main characters also change from the beginning of the book to the end. In the beginning Jerry seems friendly and direct; Mark, withdrawn and insecure. Through testing, however, Mark proves to be the one who is more perceptive and dependable. He tries to put himself in the thief's shoes by imagining what would cause him to steal. Of course, it isn't Mark's house, and the things aren't his; Lillian and Jerry focus on the objects stolen. But Lillian comes around to Mark's way of thinking and begins to consider someone else's feelings. Jerry still cannot understand why the other two are taking such a big risk by asking the strange man in. Many readers will agree more with Jerry. The boys really haven't changed so much. Lillian, it seems, has learned at least a few things: adult ways (such as drinking wine) are not as much fun as she thought; people are not always what they appear at first impression to be.

Relationships between teenagers and adults may be the most pervasive theme of this book. First, Lillian, like most 15-year-olds, doesn't understand some of the concerns or demands of her parents. She is, for example, frustrated by her parents' concern for neatness and cleanliness. Her perceptions are exaggerated (the story is told from her point of view, and 15-year-olds exaggerate). She surely does make a mess of the house, with Mark and Jerry's help, while her parents are away, and she sees that that situation won't work without someone else around to clean up after you. There is also the conflict between the three teenagers and the policeman, who fits the stereotype of the adult who is not to be trusted himself and who doesn't trust young people. Unfounded assumptions he makes about sexual misconduct and drugs build the trio's resentment toward him. What the policeman does and says contributes to the prejudices about all adults. But the inspector gains their respect by both talking with them and listening to them. The man from the woods also gives them trust by sharing something about himself. It is ironic that the one we expected to tell lies, the robber, is the adult the teenagers trust most, whereas the first policeman is the adult they trust least. Like the book as a whole, this element is too contrived. *Run* was not widely reviewed, but what comments there were tended to be negative. Linda Silver, for example, writing in *Library Journal,* criticizes Sleator's heavy-handed symbolism. She says, "The three teenage characters . . . are unappealing and seem much younger than their given ages. The story's suspenseful beginning deteriorates into a series of encounters between adversaries, the only purpose of which is to drive home the theme of the strong victimizing the weak."[5]

Even Ann Durell was not so pleased with *Run:* "Publishing is a business of hopes, and I had a lot of faith in Bill's potential as a writer. So I made many suggestions, which he more than willingly followed, and I felt the final book was acceptable, if not as strong as I would have liked." Reassuringly, a better book preceded and many more better books were to follow.

4. Science Fiction for Younger Adults: Experimenting with Nutty Paradoxes

When Sleator began to use his own imagination more and to depend less on letting his books grow out of suggestions from friends, places he had been, people he had known, and houses he had lived in, he created the bizarre, Dali-esque setting of *House of Stairs* (1974). *Into the Dream* (1979), his next science fiction book for young adults, has a UFO, mental telepathy, levitation, and psychokinesis. *The Green Futures of Tycho* (1981) features an 11-year-old protagonist involved in time travel.

House of Stairs

In the summer of 1969 Sleator was awarded a fellowship to attend the Bread Loaf Writers Conference. His name had been submitted by his former editor, Emilie McLeod. Bread Loaf is unusual in that those attending are told *not* to bring typewriters; would-be writers go there not to write but to learn. For two weeks the faculty of professional writers, the fellows, and a large number of aspiring writers live in the Green Mountain National Forest. Of the experience Sleator says:

> I'm not sure how much I learned at Bread Loaf, but it was certainly an intense experience. I came away from Bread Loaf

with the vague idea of writing a book about some teenagers in a kind of *Ship of Fools* situation, set apart from the rest of society, where the rules of behavior change. In the next few years, while I was writing *Blackbriar* and *Run,* I continued to think about this idea. I made lists of characters and decided who the five teenagers would be—one of them was me, one was a woman I had gotten to know at Bread Loaf, and the other three were high school friends of mine.

Sleator says the idea for the setting, and also the title, came from a print by M. C. Escher entitled *House of Stairs,* a print showing a place of endless stairways with segmented, wormlike little creatures crawling around on them.

At the time Sleator was beginning to get interested in the field of behavior modification. He had read B. F. Skinner's *Science and Human Behavior* and was impressed that not once did Skinner say anything he could not prove; he simply stated the results of his rigorous scientific research.

The basic idea of behaviorism is that organisms will continue to do things for which they are rewarded and will stop doing things for which they are not rewarded. Skinner trained laboratory animals to behave in specific ways simply by feeding them according to certain schedules. Sleator found these reinforcement schedules extremely interesting, especially in the way they applied to real-life situations. He decided to put five teenagers in a similar experiment. They would be trained to behave in specific ways by a machine that fed them at certain times. He picked a particular feeding schedule described by Skinner (variable ratio reinforcement in combination with a discriminative stimulus) that would result in long-lasting behavior. He was careful, throughout, to be scientifically accurate about all these things.

Sleator's intention was to write a story about the positive aspects of behavior modification. There had been several famous novels depicting behavior modification as sinister and inhuman, and he wanted to show that this was not the case at all. And so in the first draft the experiment was *good;* its object was to stimulate empathy in the subjects, to train them to be more understanding of one another.

But Sleator had a lot of problems with that draft. It had nowhere to go. He couldn't get to the end of it. He was also broke. He says, "So when I had written 100 pages or so, I sent it to Ann, hoping for a contract and an advance—and an idea for the ending. But Ann rejected it. Her reasoning was that by its nature such an experiment could not be good—if its goals were positive and humane, then the subjects would have to be volunteers; they would have to be told why they were there, and what would be done to them. And, of course, she was right. In democratic societies there are strict and necessary laws about human research."

Sleator says it is equally true that no one would want to read a story about a benevolent experiment. Actually, there would *be* no story, no credibility and interest, were the reader and the characters to know why they were there from the beginning. There could be mystery and suspense only if the characters were there against their will and ignorant of what was going to happen to them. And that meant the experiment itself, and the society that allowed it, had to be cruel and inhumane.

It made sense. As much as he didn't want to write yet another book about behavior modification used destructively, Sleator felt he hadn't much choice. And so he switched courses, changing things so that the point of the experiment was to train the young people to be cruel to one another. It was stimulating for Sleator to sit there and think up horrible things for the young people to do to one another. His intention now was to have all five go along with the experiment and be conditioned into monsters; that's what he believed would happen in real life. But once again Durell stepped in. She said she refused to publish a book for adolescents that painted such a negative picture of human nature; some of the young people had to rebel against the experiment and resist being conditioned. Sleator again gave in:

> And so, being young and malleable—not to mention broke—I once again went along with what she said, and had two of the teenagers choose to risk starvation rather than become monsters. And despite my own cynical view of human nature, I couldn't deny that it made a much better story this way— everybody likes reading about decent people fighting an inhu-

mane system. Not to mention I could still throw in all sorts of sadistic details—which I was beginning to see came very naturally to me—and at the same time appear to be making a lofty moral statement.

But he still didn't know the real purpose of the experiment. He had to have some reason for government funding, some practical goal to be achieved by training people to be cruel. Yet he didn't know what that was. Then he went to visit his parents—

probably because I was too poor to buy food—and I showed the manuscript to my mother and asked her to come up with a reason for the experiment. My mother is a good writer, and she used to help me write things when I was a kid in school. Actually, she didn't just *help* me write things; she used to write things for me, and I would hand them in as my own work—and then she would be indignant if the teacher didn't give the paper a good grade. When I was in third grade, we had to write a poem about Thanksgiving. So she wrote this great poem about Thanksgiving from the point of view of the turkey, the cranberry, and the pumpkin. And the school psychologist was so impressed by it that he published it in a book he was writing as a poem by a gifted nine-year-old. That was my mother's first publication. She now writes learned scientific papers.

Sleator says he loves telling that story to educators. His mother did come up with the reason for the experiment in *House of Stairs:* that it was sanctioned by a warlike, totalitarian society, and that its object was to train people to be without human feelings, so that they would be ideal secret agents, interrogators, and directors of concentration camps. It was a good idea, and Sleator was now able to finish the book.

To make sure everything was scientifically accurate, he showed this draft to a friend, Dr. William Redd, a professor of psychology at the University of Illinois at Urbana, where Sleator's parents now lived. Dr. Redd came up with one of the most striking ideas in the book. He suggested that one of the characters use the reinforcement techniques learned from the food machine to *help* one of the other characters, thereby demonstrating that behavior modification can be used for good as well as evil purposes. And so at one point Lola reinforces Peter for staying out of his catatonic trances. But, Sleator says, "Ann did not like this idea. I guess she thought it made the story too complicated, and that the book would be stronger if I depicted behavior modification as totally evil. But this time I refused to go along with her—I think it was the first time I balked at one of her suggestions. It was very important for me to show that behavior modification had its positive side. And eventually Ann backed down."

Finally Sleator had a contract and an advance, and after a few more revisions *House of Stairs* was published and got good reviews. People assumed it was making some kind of deeply felt statement about the human condition. The truth is that Sleator, in the interests of telling a good story, ended up seeming to express an attitude toward behavior modification that is the opposite of what he believes, and the opposite of what he had intended to say when he started it.

Most young adults experience the terrible dilemma of constant, intense pressure toward conformity and the equally intense counterpressure to affirm and maintain individual identity and integrity. *House of Stairs* raises the question of the conflict between the rewards of conformity—which can be as basic as food, acceptance, even life itself—and the satisfaction and needs of individuality. These do always, to some extent, clash. Peter and Lola demonstrate that individuality comes not just through surface characteristics but through beliefs and attitudes that influence self-affirmation and the identification of self with what is not self.

House of Stairs is the story not just of Peter and Lola but of five 16-year-old orphans who find themselves trapped in a surrealistic, nightmare setting—an endless maze of stairways, going in every direction, leading nowhere. They have been bound, blindfolded, and brought to this maze from the home for orphans for no reason they know of.

Peter is submissive when the blindfold and ropes are taken off: "Shaking, he sank to his knees at the base of a flight of steps leading up from the landing. He wrapped his arms around himself and dropped his head onto his chest, closing his eyes, and tried his best not to move, or think." Of course, he wonders why he is here. Is it forever? Can he escape? The nightmarish stairs and his own fears and inadequacies cause him increasingly to lapse into inaction and daydreams. He reminds us of Danny in *Blackbriar,* in that respect. When he dreams, he dreams of Jasper, a friend who took care of him in one of the orphan's homes in the past.

When Peter comes out of his dream, Lola is there, with her rough voice, tough talk, and tomboy ways. Peter at first thinks she is a boy. She is more aggressive, but she does not know anything about why they are there either. Lola, however, is not going to be passive about it. She looks at Peter with a "penetrating" gaze. Lola is frightening to Peter. She regards him as "one of those shy, sensitive creeps . . . who never wanted to have any fun because he was always afraid of getting caught." That Lola has never given in to authority or obeyed rules could be the reason she is here. But what would explain Peter's presence?

Peter at first gives in to hopelessness, but Lola persuades him to help her seek a way out. They don't find it, and Peter allows himself to fall into his dream of Jasper much more frequently. Lola is able to maintain faith in her ability to survive.

Blossom is the next character to be introduced. Peter and Lola find her sitting in front of the machine. It spits out a cylinder of meat each time she sticks out her tongue spitefully. Two more 16-year-olds, Abigail and Oliver, arrive at the machine, but it does not respond to them. A day or so later (there is no clock or sunlight to tell when a day passes) the machine begins flashing an intense red light, accompanied by whispering voices. Accidentally the five find a series of moves that cause the machine to give up a small ball of food. They repeat the moves and are again rewarded. They will be fed when they dance! But the dance must please the machine, and the machine is not always consistent. It never yields enough food, either, and so they learn to dance urgently every time the lights flash and the voices whisper. Food comes only if *all* dance.

The characters are developed further. Blossom is fat, selfish, and spoiled; she is a manipulator and knows how to hate, especially Lola. Oliver is a handsome, happy-go-lucky jock who wants to be the leader but has trouble filling the role. Peter is attracted to him in an almost-sexual way, but mostly as a replacement for Jasper. Oliver is flattered by this sort of hero worship: "He shifted on the step, and Peter looked up at him for a moment, wide-eyed. It had been rather unexpected to find himself almost at once the object of Peter's intense devotion, but Oliver didn't mind. It made him feel confident and powerful to have someone look up to him so much. Although, down at the bottom of it, something about Peter gnawed at him." Oliver does not allow the others to wake Peter, but otherwise he shows little concern for him. He uses Abigail, because he knows she is attracted to him, by leading her away for necking sessions but immediately afterward turns cold and aloof. He fears Lola because he knows she is strong.

Abigail is weak and does not want competitiveness to develop in the group: "To Abigail, who was always considering what boys thought of her, or what the other girls in her group would think, who was always trying to avoid doing whatever might hurt someone, or make her disliked, Lola's behavior was hard to understand. It made Abigail, in some strange way, feel trapped; trapped, and then resentful of Lola's freedom."

Blossom, manipulator that she is, sways both Oliver and Abigail to her side in the battle for food, and that makes her ready one day when the machine begins to do unusual things. At first when the lights blink and the voices whisper, the youths dance and food rolls out. But on repetition of the dance, no more food appears. Oliver speculates that the machine is trying to teach them something new. Frustrated, Lola runs off, and Blossom, taking advantage of her not being there, tells the others things Lola has said about them, lying as much as she needs to. Lola returns and discovers what has been going on. She is enraged, shakes her head at Blossom, and asks Blossom if she realizes what she is doing. Lola says, "You're hurting *them* just as much as me. . . . You don't give a shit about another living thing, do you? All you care about is your own fat self, and so you go around in this unhuman way *betraying* people." At this, the lights begin flashing, the voices come on, the teenagers begin to dance, and food pellets roll—the machine likes for them to hurt one another. Lola is intensely bothered by this development: to eat, she will have to violate all her convictions.

Peter then takes an assertive action of the kind he has never before taken—he offers to help Lola resist the machine. But now he finds it troublesome that someone will be *depending* on him in the way he has previously depended on Lola, and so he retreats into his trance. Lola, however, uses positive reinforcement to bring him out of it. When Peter and Lola go to tell the others that they are going to resist the machine, Lola cannot help yielding to the machine's signals to dance. Peter is strong enough not only to resist but to pull Lola away. Over time, without food, their interdependence grows as their physical strength dwindles.

The other three become less human as the machine forces them to prey on one another. Ultimately, Lola knows she is near death and that her will to live is stronger than her will to resist the machine. Although Peter no longer has any desire to stay alive, he agrees to give in because he knows Lola could not give in alone. Just in time, however, the authorities arrive to take them out of the house of stairs.

Eventually, after rest and recuperation, the five find out they have been part of a government experiment. Blossom, Abigail, and Oliver have passed, and they are to complete their tests before being sent away for advanced training. Peter and Lola have failed. In the last scene, a real chiller, Blossom, Abigail, and Oliver—returned to the everyday world—begin to dance at the sight of a blinking green traffic light.

Major themes here are the horrors of operant conditioning, good versus evil, and freedom versus conformity. Sleator dedicates the book "to all the rats and pigeons who have already been there." He also wrote a book on behavior modification with William H. Redd, *Taking Charge: A Personal Guide to Behavior Modification*. Even today behavioral scientists are performing experiments like those in *House of Stairs*. The subjects are usually pigeons, rats, and dogs, but people have sometimes been used for tests by their governments and employers. Behavioral modification is used by institutions of authority all the time, but in more subtle ways than in this novel—so subtle that we often don't realize we are being manipulated, conditioned to respond in certain ways. Just as the young people in the story are unable to see the scientists or even realize they are the subjects of experimentation, we often do not see those who manipulate us. Many times those in charge do not realize that is what they are doing, but the experiments go on all the same—by government, the media, and even schools.

Pamela D. Pollack, reviewer for *Library Journal,* relates this theme of the book to contemporary political events: "The Post-Watergate propagandizing (the President was in on the experiment which was supposed to turn out operatives who would follow unquestioningly any order given to them and not get caught) will not be too obvious for teens, nor will they be put off by the graphic violence and animalistic acts in what is primarily an intensely suspenseful page-turner par excellence."[1]

Good versus evil plays a large part here, despite Sleator's insistence that he does not believe in such abstractions. The struggle between good and evil in *House of Stairs* is not abstract; it is quite concrete. The chief experimenter, for instance, is shrouded in the kind of evil that dims vision and clouds judgment. He is opposed by the good in characters like Lola and Peter.

Another main theme is freedom of the individual in a society that values conformity. Here it is food that is the motivator; in society, more often it is money. Lola and Peter show that the way to defeat the pressure to conform is to deny the positive reinforcer. A tough thing to do, but it is the only way to start on the way toward freedom.

The setting of *House of Stairs* is a place full of steps going endlessly up and down and out and over in all directions–no walls, no floor, no ceiling, no windows, just stairs: "All he could see were stairs. The high, narrow landing on which he stood seemed to be the only flat place there was, and above and below him, growing smaller in the distance, were only flights of steps. Without railings they rose and fell at alarming angles, forking, occasionally spiraling, rising briefly together only to veer apart again, crossing above and below one another, connecting at rare intervals by thin bridges spanning deep gulfs."

There is no point of reference, no idea as to which way to go. The stairs above and below are increasingly hard to reach. The stairs to which the teenagers have access lead nowhere. Chaos, so intriguing to Sleator, is hinted at here: stairs that seemingly go on forever but could divide and yet lead nowhere. Most of this story deals with order, but it is an imposed order, one the experimenters are trying to create by means of their behavioral-conditioning experiments. This order (or perhaps it is a change of order) has horrible consequences, and those who manage to rebel against it are the heroes of the book.

Critical opinion has been almost universally favorable, with comments like these: "The brutalization of human guinea pigs is a Skinnerian experiment in terror. Topflight SF/suspense,"[2] and "extremely interesting, uncomfortable novel. . . . Mr. Sleator is saying some deep things here about privacy and courage and the rights of the individual; he's not a bit simplistic either."[3] The book might even be called a passion, a cult book, among many young adult readers and librarians. Many critics agree that it is by far Sleator's best book to date.

Into the Dream

Into the Dream uses a UFO as a plot device. This novel is Sleator's second science fiction effort for younger adults, and here he truly reaches his stride in appealing to those readers. Sleator says the idea for this book came from a nightmare he had about two people having the same dream. Thinking there might be a story there, he sat down to write in order to see what would happen. He came up with a highly supernatural tale, one full of ambiguity and rejected by Ann Durell. Sleator put it aside for awhile. He recalls:

> Then one day when I was seriously broke, I got the manuscript out again. I kept the original idea and threw out everything else. In the interests of trying to come up with a salable story as quickly as possible, I did something I had never tried before: I sat down and worked out the whole plot—beginning, middle,

and end—before I started actually writing. I knew Ann wouldn't like the book unless I came up with an airtight reason for these kids having the same dream—and looking for an explanation that would satisfy her was what led to a workable plot.

He was amazed at what a difference it made to plan out the book before writing it. The work went much faster than any of his other books; he came up with a completely new manuscript in a few months, rather than a year. And for the first time Ann Durell bought a book on the basis of what was essentially a first draft. Sleator decided from then on to plan out all his novels in advance. Although the idea seems pretty obvious to Sleator now, he had to learn it from firsthand experience.

The story involves Paul, a sensitive, intelligent boy, and his bright, tough classmate Francine. The two discover they have been bothered, even frightened, by the same dream, a nightmare so filled with urgent messages that it has become an obsession. In the dream there is a third person, a little boy in white pajamas. The nightmare progresses nightly and drives Paul and Francine to a feeling of impending doom for the little boy. These two have, to say the least, not been close friends before; they have not even been compatible. But to help save the boy and themselves, they develop a bond. Their cooperation leads to the discovery that they both possess powers of telepathic communication as a result of their exposure to a UFO.

As to how that UFO explanation came about, and commenting on Sleator's revision strategies, Ann Durell writes, "*Into the Dream's* quality makes it a good example of Bill's great gift for revision; as I recall the first version lacked any explanation of the ESP and other powers of Paul, Francine, Noah, and Cookie. I pointed out to Bill that the story needed what Alfred Hitchcock called the McGuffin—the device that triggers and propels the plot. He went off and, as always, came up with the perfect answer to the problem—the UFO."

It turns out that the dream figure in the white pajamas is Noah Jaleela and that he has a dog named Cookie. Cookie is responsible for Paul and Francine's dream, because she is concerned about Noah and wants help. Noah is also telepathic and possesses psychokinetic abilities. Piecing the story together, Paul and Francine find Noah and Cookie and discover that the government wants to exploit Noah's powers and use him as a secret weapon. Their attempt to save Noah leads to the climax of the story, in which Paul and Noah levitate above a carnival Ferris wheel. Everyone gains something positive from the experience (except the government bad guys).

The plot is complex and intricate—some might even say contrived—but does work well to show the evolving relationship between Paul and Francine. As they learn more about the meaning of the dream, they come to respect each other more. Francine sees herself as superior, and Paul sees her this way also. Although he does not enjoy her domination, when he wakes up one night shuddering and shaking and dripping with sweat, barely able to keep from "crying out in anguish," he realistically concludes that he has no choice but to join her to avert the terror. She makes him feel dull and inferior, yet he knows it "really was Francine who had most of the ideas and who always seemed to know what to do."

That Paul and Francine work well as a team become clear when the two government agents who have been following them come to Paul's house. Fearing what might happen if they are seen, the youngsters are able wordlessly to communicate the need for caution to Paul's mother. After they have got away safely, Paul feels Francine has been brilliant in her performance, and Francine "almost seems to respect him now." By the book's conclusion they have both matured in general and in their respect for and understanding of each other. When the Ferris wheel seat Paul and Noah are riding in breaks loose at one corner, Noah uses psychokinesis to hold it level and even tears the whole seat free so that the two float in it above the Ferris wheel. Paul tries to broadcast by telepathy to Francine that all will be well. When he and Noah ride the Ferris wheel seat back down to earth, Francine tells him, "If something had happened to you I don't know what I would do," and Paul replies, "It was you that saved us." (Francine had managed to get the TV camera operators and reporters on the scene, despite the attempts of the government agents to keep them away.)

The slow, suspenseful uncovering of the various links in the dream is ingenious. The book is both a science fiction thriller and an action-packed mystery in which Paul and Francine piece together the puzzle offered by all the various clues. For instance, the dream itself: Why are they having similar recurring nightmares? Part of the mystery is the source of the dream—the identity of the little boy, the meaning of the word *stardust,* the "dark hulking creature," and the glowing sphere in the middle of the field. And then there are the questions about the future: What are the motives of the two men, and what are they going to do? When will this awful thing happen? How can they prevent whatever it is from coming to pass?

As Paul and Francine answer more of these questions, as they use their sense of mental telepathy, their powers expand, and so does the plot. This is the way Sleator almost always works with plot. He begins in the known, real world, "a situation with which the reader can identify," and "then sneaks in the unreal elements" ("SF," 5). Note how he allows Paul and Francine to discover and expand their psychic gifts, which they first learn about when Paul knows by telepathy which house is Francine's and that her parents are divorced; in the same way, Francine knows that Paul can't stand the sound of cracked ice. Before long they discover they can send messages to each other mentally, but not always clearly. Not long after that, they learn to communicate without talking. Finally, with expanded senses Paul can receive feelings from many of the people in the crowd during the Ferris wheel scene.

As he frequently does, Sleator leaves the ending of the book somewhat open. Countless future adventures with Francine, Paul, Noah, and Cookie could occur. At the end of the book they are again receiving unspoken messages from Cookie as she sleeps. Another book could follow on the same subject. Are they going to be famous? studied? exploited? Like Paul, we wonder what they are going to dream that night.

Sleator uses settings-within-settings. Here the main plot is in a city. The school and the downtown area of the city are clearly described, as are Paul's middle-class house and Francine's dingy, lower-class apartment building. The setting-within-the-setting is the dream experience that takes us to Reno and the Stardust Motel. While hazy at first, the setting becomes progressively clearer through added detail as the dreams continue and the characters converse. The black-and-white illustrations by Ruth Sanderson in the hardcover edition are especially good at capturing the dreamlike quality of Sleator's descriptions of place. They are really more black than white, very shadowy, and this quality is appropriate for the atmosphere of the work.

Sleator subtly presents his characters in nontraditional gender roles. Paul's mother is a scientist. Whereas Francine is portrayed as aggressive and intelligent, Paul has many of the traits traditionally associated with women. Paul is a good student, a favorite of his teacher. He does not repress but expresses his fears. In dream sequences he is described as "tense with fear," awakening to "the sound of his own cry in the dark bedroom, the terror still with him." He also has much consideration for the feelings of others. Although both he and Francine are competitive about which one of them is smarter, Paul is not aggressive in this. Francine is much more forthright in her criticism of Paul's "incompetence." Paul is more introspective. He does not retaliate when Francine complains about his inability to rescue anybody. He knows Francine is resourceful, willing to take risks, and headstrong.

The family unit is not important in this novel—all three of the children are from single-parent homes. To some extent Paul's and Francine's mothers are controlled by their children through mental telepathy. It is significant that Paul does not tell his mother his dreams: "He did not want her to laugh it off as something psychological, as he knew she would." He also knew his mother would say ESP did not exist.

Because Paul and Francine think adults will not believe them, they take matters into their own hands. They don't tell Noah's mother, Mrs. Jaleela, the truth about their inquiry, even after she says she trusts them: "She'll think we're crazy." Nor do they in-form the police. Miss Keck, Paul and Francine's teacher, is presented as an obstacle to their plan. She has little sympathy for Paul. Her only response to his seeming preoccupation is to threaten to call his mother to tell her Paul's work is falling off. Of course, she has not even a hint about the earthshaking problems Paul is having, but neither does she attempt to find an explanation for his behavior.

The government, as represented by the CIA, is presented in an unfavorable light. At the end it tries to prevent Noah's powers from being filmed for television. The CIA is portrayed as evil not because it is adult but because it exploits and dehumanizes. A moral lesson is subtly given: many people want to take advantage of innocents like Noah; thus, watch out for them.

Two animals play roles in the story. The dog Rose, who is the mother of Cookie, is pregnant and in the Reno area the night of the UFO landing there. Because of this prenatal influence, Cookie, the offspring, later plays a major role. She has well-developed ESP powers and is the cause of Paul and Francine's dreams. Since Cookie has received these unique powers as a result of her mother's exposure to the UFO, what about the other puppies in the litter? Are there other dogs who can communicate mentally with people? Cookie's concern for Noah,and apparent knowledge of the danger he is in, is the reason for her contact with Paul and Francine. It is her plan to leave the apartment after the arrival of the CIA. She also tries to warn against the amusement park, but nobody will listen to her. (And it's a good thing they don't, for we would not have had the best scene in the book, and one of the best scenes in all Sleator's work—a cliff-hanger, or rather a Ferris wheel–hanger, that grips the reader from start to finish).

Language is particularly important in this book. The speech of the two 12-year-olds is especially authentic. Sleator is able to distinguish between the voices of Paul, an above-average student who studies all the time, and Francine,an average student who characterizes Paul as "silly." Whereas Paul uses little slang, Francine frequently does so—with such phrases as "brain boy." Mrs. Jaleela's inadequacies of expression and inability to cope are shown vividly. By contrast, Noah has the ability to speak his thoughts on a more enriched level than a typical four-year-old. Note his last expression in the book: "So nice . . . Cookie not worried any more. She's been worrying for so long, but now it's over. And now I have you too, Paul and Francine. So nice . . . the way you can understand me . . . so nice."

This novel is written for children around or just below the middle-school level. Several reviews agreed on ages 9 to 13 for this book. The writing style is not too complicated, and readers may pick up a new word here and there, such as *rapt, gamboling, rankling,* and *languid.* The narrative style is sometimes overly descriptive, as with the portrayal of the nervous Mrs. Jaleela (her incessant smoking, her shaky handwriting on the door, her poor memory, her tremors), but it is always easy to follow. Some of the descriptive passages are vivid and add to the story's excitement.

Reviewers of *Into the Dream* have used such phrases as "Swiftly paced and very readable,"[4] "ESP and psychokinesis thrill the readers,"[5] and "Tightly woven suspense and an ingenious, totally involving plot line . . . make this a thriller of top-notch quality."[6] They have also been critical. Pamela Pollack was particularly scathing: "Sleator doesn't miss a marketplace with this gallimaufry of UFO's, ESP, even the CIA . . . all of this is hard to take strictly on Sleator's say-so, and he barely manages to make it all mesh."[7]

Opinion on the illustrations is somewhat divided too. *Language Arts* said the nine black-and-white framed drawings "neither add nor detract from Sleator's highly charged novel."[8] *Reading Teacher,* on the other hand, praised them: "Intricate black pencil drawings add substance to the eerie, nebulous content of the dream."[9]

Possibly the book's editor, Ann Durell, comes closest to the mark in a recent letter. Having just reread *Into the Dream,* she remarked, "I was struck anew by what a well-crafted book it is. Everything works—nothing is introduced just for suspense purposes and all of the elements of the fantasy are convincingly explained. It's top-notch Sleator, right down to the twist of 'This is not all over: what next?' at the end, which has become almost a trademark of his books."

The Green Futures of Tycho

The Green Futures of Tycho is the first of several books in which time travel is possible, multiple selves are created, and sibling rivalries are of major importance. Sleator continues to make his young protagonist instrumental in saving the world from possible chaos, as in *Into the Dream.* So too does he continue to explore the possibility of parallel or possible worlds-within-worlds, as in *House of Stairs, Among the Dolls,* and *Once, Said Darlene.*

Names are very important in this book—not only the first names of the children, who are named for famous people, but also their last name, Tithonus, which comes from Greek mythology. (Remember, Sleator's grandmother read Greek.) Tithonus had immortality but not eternal youth. By possessing a time device, Tycho will be able to become immortal—and make his family immortal if he so chooses—if not eternally young. The older Tycho uses the device to control his life span and is eventually destroyed, just as Tithonus eventually shriveled up and was turned into a grasshopper.

The book opens in the prehistoric world of a brontosaurus that sees a being drop an object but is oblivious to it. Several million years later, the object is dug up by 11-year-old Tycho Tithonus when he is spading a vegetable garden in his backyard. When Tycho picks it up and puts it in his pocket, he begins an adventure in time travel.

Sleator doesn't know how he conceived the one-page opening chapter of this book. When Ann Durell read the first draft, she said it was the best first page he had ever written. Unfortunately, the rest of this draft did not live up to the potential of the opening—it was an unworkable story about an alien egg that hatches an organism the protagonist has to nurture to adulthood—and Durell rejected it.

Sleator was back on page 1. He had to come up with another explanation for this alien object, dropped on the earth millennia ago. And then he thought, Time travel! Time travel had always been one of his favorite science fiction subjects. Having learned from the experience of *Into the Dream,* he brainstormed, came up with a good time-travel story, wrote the book in about a month, and sent it to Durell, who accepted it. Further, she asked for fewer revisions than he ever believed possible. Sleator had finally learned how to write a book. He says, "From now on, I thought, all novels would be as effortless. Of course, this prediction did not turn out to be accurate."

Tycho's older brothers' and sister's lives are filled with lessons and practice and more lessons, to live up to the names of the famous people they were named for and to fulfill their parents' expectations. Sixteen-year-old Ludwig Tithonus was named for the German composer Ludwig van Beethoven; 15-year-old Tamara Tithonus was named for a Russian dancer, Tamara Karsavina; and 13-year-old Leonardo Tithonus was named after the Italian artist and inventor Leonardo da Vinci.

The youngest, Tycho, named for the famous Danish astronomer Tycho Brahe, is 11, and he does not fit into the pattern his parents have made for him. He is not interested in stars anymore than he is interested in trees, or dinosaurs, or plants, and he will not take lessons after school. The three older children pick on him, and the parents side with the older children against him: "His parents, and his brothers and sister, had never liked him very much." (Sleator dedicates this book to his brother Tycho, who was the baby of the family.)

By accident when he is quarreling with his siblings over the object he has found, Tycho presses one end of it and everyone disappears and just as suddenly reappears. But the whole day has miraculously passed in those few seconds.

Tycho next deliberately tries to learn how to use the object to travel in time again. He notices that its appearance changes constantly. When he picks it up in the yard it is just silver. The next time he looks at it, the silver oval, the size of a small egg, seems to have visible lines like dials on one end, and the opposite end to have a greenish tint to it. When he returns from his trip out of time, the object is warm to the touch. The next time he looks at it the markings are clearer and more complex and the end glows. At the next inspection he discovers the markings are concentric circles and are actually dials he can move.

Tycho travels into several futures before he finds his older self, who shows him how to use the time machine. The next day Tycho goes five years into the past to stop the older children from tormenting his six-year-old self. Upon return from that trip he can no longer fit the egg into his pants pocket. It has grown. The egg has changed: "The green end had become sharply faceted, like a jewel, and the color was more intense than it had been. The dials were clearer now. They no longer looked etched in metal, but had dimension and relief. And wrapped around the middle of the egg was a thin glittering filament."

Tycho uses the egg to go 20 years into the future and is disgusted at the way his adult self behaves in general and at how cruel he is to Tamara. On his return he notices the egg has changed again. This time "the green end was more jewel like than before, with a richer, warmer glow. It had a mysterious underwater quality now, that was quite hypnotic. . . . And around the middle there were two glittering filaments: one silver and the other red." He persuades Leonardo to side with him by offering to show him how to disappear at will. The feeling of power at being able to make his family do what he wants just by changing a few things in the past is intoxicating—until he tries another trip into what he thinks is the same future 20 years ahead, and three and a half hours later. But instead he is in an entirely different future, one he is less happy to see. Leonardo is now an enormous, 659-pound creature floating in weightless space in a huge, padded circular room in a satellite in orbit around the earth, and keeps in contact with Tycho by phone—when Tycho chooses to take his calls. The 11-year-old Tycho is appalled by this new possible future he sees ahead of him.

During dinner, the answer to why these two futures were possible comes to him: "The future, after all, was not already determined, like the past. It was still liquid and flowing, becoming solid only as each instant happened. Of course, character and personality had something to do with how things turned out. But so did chance, the unpredictable element. Because of chance, there were endless possibilities. *Which meant that each person had many different possible futures.*" Tycho keeps meeting himself both as a small child and as several adults. He is beginning to realize that any change in the past can change the future in some quite-unforeseen ways.

Ludwig tries to force Tycho to show him the egg, and while struggling over it Tycho sends himself back 45 minutes into the past. His reaction to holding the egg again is a caressing, delicious sensation. Now, however, there are two eggs—the one Ludwig sees 45 minutes into the future and the one Tycho is holding. Tycho kicks the other one into the closet and now the future will change one more time. He tells Ludwig that in the future he will have some awful disease, an announcement that crushes the older boy.

The egg has changed again. This time shapes are moving inside the green crystal. Around the egg are three bands of little glittering cells (filaments) of silver, red, and gold, with tiny blinking lights: "Clearly the egg was becoming increasingly active. . . . But he didn't want to think about what the activity might mean. He was getting better and better at avoiding things."

Tycho again travels almost 20 years into the future, and this is an even more bizarre time. He has to use the egg to unlock the door so that he can get inside the house. The Tycho who lives in this future is a tyrant who physically and mentally tortures his three siblings. Leonardo is forced to make sculptures of spiky, anemonelike green creatures that are covered with veiny, wrinkled lumps and snoutlike protuberances and have several gaping, thick-lipped mouths. Ludwig is forced to play a strange instrument that Tycho thinks might be a broadcasting device. And Tamara is forced to use the egg to make copies of itself. This older Tycho wears a green plastic mask to hide an ugly black stain like a birthmark across his face: "It was his soul, printed on his face." The 11-year-old Tycho is so upset by this future that when he returns safely to the past, he throws up. This future self was a "demented monster who had turned the rest of his family into slaves."

Now the "pictures inside the jewel shifted and changed. The beehive of cells now reached from the jewel to the dials, flickering on and off in busy, complex patterns."

Tycho thinks there must be some future that is a good one, and so he tries one more time. This time the older Tycho, who has "little green growths sprouting out of the stain on his face," takes the egg from him. This older Tycho says this ruined world is what "they" want, that this is what "they" told him to do. This mysterious "they" will be here soon, since he has opened the way for them. Tycho finally figures out that the one connecting link among all these future worlds is the egg—the time machine. How can he take it back and drop it where they will never find it?

Each "future Tycho" is worse than the last, until the final older Tycho, who, amazingly enough, is almost the same in the last two visits to the future. Tycho remembers the egg he had kicked into the closet in one of those pasts. With it he escapes into the past, with the older Tycho close behind. The egg has become more complex and versatile and now seems to have a homing device in it to trace energy from other eggs. In his escape back through the past Tycho comes across himself several times, including the first time he interfered with the past when the six-year-old Tycho was being tormented by the three older children. Tycho had gone back in time deliberately to this very scene in his first conscious time travel—his first interference in the past to change the future. And at the end of the book, here he is again in the same scene as he tries to get rid of the egg for good.

Tycho manages to go back to the time when the beings dropped the thing—or did they deliberately plant it? His older self is suffocating him in the mud when Tycho manages to make the final jump into the past. He puts the egg in his mouth while he searches for the original dropped object, which seems to wriggle away from him in the mud and to squirm out of his fingers before he gets a good grip on it. The future Tycho is blinked out of existence when the original egg is returned to the alien's pouch, as is the 11-year-old Tycho, who was created by his first visit into the past to change things. The Tycho in the epilogue is one who was never affected by the egg, because it was never left behind—or was it?

The epilogue repeats the beginning of chapter 2, with a new twist. Instead of putting his find into his pocket, Tycho gives it to

Tamara, who is helping him. Has this present been affected by something in the past, since both Tycho and Tamara now share the gardening project? Is it possible that the sibling rivalry will no longer be three against one but will instead result in a happier life for all the family and none of the futures Tycho visited?

The object Tycho has found this time is actually an old lipstick tube. When he found the egg the first time he had lied to his siblings, telling them it was just an old lipstick tube that he had then lost: "Something stirred deep inside his brain, something unpleasant. What had made him start to put it in his pocket?" When he says he would like for summer to be over in one second so that they could be eating the tomatoes right now, Tamara answers him that summer will go by fast enough: "It always does." Tycho happily goes back to digging. But why does he feel so happy?

Throughout the book, Sleator has referred to the time machine as an egg. It seems to be alive, wiggling and squirming as Tycho tries to return the newly planted object to the alien's pouch. Each time Tycho uses the original egg it changes, growing larger, becoming more complex, gaining powers. Finally, the reader realizes that its use could so corrupt the world as to make life a chaotic mess vulnerable to alien takeover. The egg was a seed that had been deliberately planted by these three creatures, each with "veiny, wrinkled bumps on its body, and little snoutlike protuberances."

The parents play only a minor role in this story. They are both physicians, want their children to call them Bobby and Judy, and are determined their offspring will become what they want them to be. They appear in most of the possible futures either as worn-out, overworked professionals or as healthy, tanned old people. Bobby can be a whiny old man, and Judy can even defend Tycho as her favorite child.

The house in *The Green Futures of Tycho* is similar to the one Sleator grew up in near St. Louis. Most of the action takes place in the house and yard. Only once does the 11-year-old Tycho venture out into the city in search of a future Tycho. The house remains a stable fixture throughout Tycho's visits to other futures.

It changes with each visit, becoming more and more modernistic and bizarre until Tycho's final visit to the future, when there is little of the actual house left but a mess. The air has a rotten smell; the new addition sags, with holes in the roof. The roof is totally gone from the original house, the exterior wall has crumpled, the interior is full of broken glass and rubble, and there are little fires flickering here and there. Enough of the original house is left to allow Tycho to battle his way up broken stairs, through piles of rubble, and over missing floorboards to the closet that holds the first duplicate egg.

Sleator again uses the idea of time travel in *Strange Attractors*, in which his characters are just as reluctant to give up their time machines as Tycho is to give up the silver egg. Just as each older version of Tycho is a little different and a little more cruel, so too are the copies of David in *The Duplicate*. One of Tycho's older selves has ugly green growths on his face; David's copies also have a blemish, one identifying them as duplicates. Tycho is chased by an older self who wants to destroy him before he has a chance to change the past. This nightmarish theme of characters being pursued by another version of themselves is a recurring one of Sleator's. David in *The Duplicate* is in danger of being destroyed by a duplicate of himself. In *Strange Attractors*, the chaotic Eve and Sylvan are trying to eliminate the real Eve and Sylvan.

About *The Green Futures of Tycho* Sleator says, "With each book I've written, my dependence upon reality has gradually diminished. As I have, ever so slowly, become more skilled at writing, I have been able to let my imagination go wilder, and get more of that down on paper. *The Green Futures of Tycho*, for example, does bear a slight tangential relationship to my own upbringing. But the real meat of the book—time travel and an attempted alien takeover of the earth—did not really happen to me."[10]

Even though Sleator and his brother-in-law thought *The Green Futures of Tycho* was funny, reviewers felt differently. Pamela Pollack in the *School Library Journal* says, "Sleator's expert blend of future and horror fiction is unusually stark, dark and intriguing; and the breakneck pace he sets never falters."[11] Neil Philip in the *Times Educational Supplement* also sees the darker side of Sleator's work. He reviews four Sleator novels: *The Boy Who Reversed Himself, House of Stairs, Singularity,* and *The Green Futures of Tycho.* He says all four "explore moral dilemmas in extreme circumstances. They confront basic questions about the universe, time and human nature. They are unflinching in their acceptance of the possibility of evil . . . but none is without hope." Philip concludes with the statement that "readers with a taste for strong-minded science fiction which is based on ideas, not hardware, will find him both challenging and rewarding."[12]

Ann Durell says that the second draft of the manuscript for *The Green Futures of Tycho* arrived in nearly perfect form and that very little revision was necessary: "Even the style was new—more polished and elegant, as befitted the sophisticated Tithonus family. My only hard work was double-checking every detail of the incredibly complicated plot. It was the first of Bill's complex books—the ones that fully demonstrate his truly amazing intelligence. I never cease to marvel at the mind that can not only understand scientific principles like the fourth dimension or period doubling but use them in a way that is accurate and also clear to the least scientific reader (which I consider myself to be!) in a highly imaginative and readable story."

5. In and out of Science Fiction

Sleator departed from science fiction in *Fingers* (1983), although it contains some strange happenings that are not entirely explained. The book tells the story of Humphrey, a former child-prodigy pianist who loses the attention of the public when he reaches puberty. The rest of the family includes his mother, Bridget; his father, Luc; and his half-brother, Sam, who is the narrator. Then there is Lazlo, the mysterious old man who becomes family later.

Because audiences no longer accept Humphrey's playing, Bridget has difficulty getting bookings for him. The virtuosity that was amazing from a child is merely second-rate from an adult. The resulting financial loss has to be remedied. Bridget comes up with what she thinks is a perfect scheme to win audiences back for Humphrey: the spirit of the Hungarian classical composer Lazlo Magyar will visit Humphrey while he is asleep and give him new compositions. Sam is forced to compose these "genuine" musical scores secretly; Bridget and Luc drug Humphrey while Sam slips the music he has composed into his hands; and Humphrey, on awakening, is told that the ghost of Magyar is sending him the music. Humphrey believes he has somehow written the music he is holding when he wakes up. He is able to play these "genuine" compositions with a flair and emotion he has never before shown, and because he plays the new music so well the family is able to resume traveling around Europe for concerts.

Sam is bothered by the joke he is playing on Humphrey, and by other weird happenings. An old man follows them around from concert to concert. No one pays much attention to him except Sam, who is extremely upset by his presence. The old man makes sure Sam finds and reads a biography of Magyar. In it Sam discovers the fact that the composer's body was buried without his head or hands. Humphrey, who never reads, to Sam's amazement begins to talk about a pair of shriveled human hands wrapped in rags. Then a pair of doll's hands wrapped in rags mysteriously appears on Humphrey's bed. Something unusual is obviously going on.

It turns out that the old man is Magyar's only child and bears his name. He has original pieces of music identical to the ones Sam has composed. Sam confesses the deception to Humphrey. Bridget and Luc follow the boys to the old man's apartment, where Bridget burns what she believes are the original scores, hoping their scheme will not be found out. The boys run away with old Lazlo and are living with him at the end of the novel. It is more than a little unmotivated that these two teens would go off with this unusual, seedy old man without fear or even second thoughts. But the whole plot contains a farcical element.

Sam's ability to compose works identical note for note with those written by Lazlo Magyar years before can be explained only by some kind of ghostly influence. Humphrey's unusual ability to play the compositions effortlessly must also come from the late Magyar. The two brothers complement each other in that together they have the most important parts and talents of the dead Hungarian composer. Remember that Lazlo Magyar was buried without his hands and head. Could they be influencing the two boys? The mystery is not resolved by the end of the novel; rather, it is further heightened by the disclosure that since their arrival on Magyar's island, the boys have begun speaking Hungarian in their sleep, although they have never been able to speak that language before. What might happen next? The reader is left to imagine the further adventures of Sam and Humphrey led on by the ghost of Lazlo Magyar.

Humphrey is a caricature of the preoccupied musician, unaware of what goes on around him. He is a prisoner of his music. He has little personality either in general or in his playing style. He originally admires Sam because he is older and protects him; however, Bridget corrupts Humphrey, and later he does not behave well toward Sam. Humphrey is unaware not only of Bridget's plot but of Sam's affection for him, and he is oblivious to the fact that his father and mother care more for him as a commodity than for him as a son. Not until Humphrey realizes Bridget and Luc's scheme does he make amends to Sam.

Sam is undergoing a kind of identity crisis. He is troubled, introverted, and in some ways brilliant. Because tutors have been hired for Sam, he is better educated than Humphrey. He has begun to question who he is and how he fits into things. Although he regrets having no father around, he is proud of the African genes his father did pass on to him and pleased he bears no resemblance to Humphrey or Luc. Sam is under the thumb of the family, but he wants to assert himself.

At first Sam thinks of Humphrey as a thing: "the only safe and sane way to deal with this object is to feel nothing about it at all." Part of this feeling is motivated by jealousy; his hands are not as large as Humphrey's, a situation that keeps him from being a great piano player. Yet Sam still has enough concern for his half-brother to ask Bridget to let Humphrey stop performing so that he can begin to live a normal life. He shows real affection when Humphrey runs away. Sam is the one who takes the lead in defying Bridget, although he is usually reserved. He is also the one who gets himself and Humphrey to the security of the old man's protection, away from the tyranny of Bridget and into—or so we are led to believe—a stable home with a father substitute.

Both Bridget and Luc are exploitive and greedy. Bridget possesses skill as a blackmailer and uses it often. She coddles Humphrey but denies Sam any mothering whatsoever. Luc is controlled by her and forces Humphrey to practice long hours. He never thinks for himself and seldom acts rationally. Even though he has a musical background, Luc lacks the talent to be a professional. He is a spineless person who follows in the direction he is pointed. He is useless as a father but quite useful as a scapegoat.

Setting is handled so as to remind us that Sam and Humphrey are always "going, going, and still going" to the next city to play without thanks. They are teenagers unable to do teenage things. *Fingers* opens in the midfifties of this century in Venice, in a dreary hotel that has seen better days. The atmosphere is bleak. Because the group is always on the road, the setting changes in different scenes, but the hotels are much alike. The theaters in which Humphrey plays have the same seedy quality. Sleator is especially apt with these descriptive passages because of all the years he spent traveling with the ballet company; he is able to describe not only the physical setting but also the general ambience of being on the road. The family spends most of its time indoors, whether in Venice, Milan, Geneva, or Cleveland. Sleator chooses not to describe these areas in great detail; instead, he saves his major descriptions for more intriguing places, such as Magyar's apartment: "The style of the decor remained consistent: more junk blackened by the grime of decades, more tattered piles of books and papers, more peeling wallpaper and rags and crumbling plaster. Only here there was an old upright piano instead of a bed, its black enameled finish blistered and cracked . . . falling apart volumes of music, except for the space occupied by a large cylindrical glass jar, sealed with a cork. The pale objects floating inside were obscured by a thick coat of dust on the glass."

The boys are happy on the island, where the house provides an escape from the otherwise-all-encompassing task of music. This sheltered place for relief from the hectic pace of show business was something never provided by Bridget and Luc. In this home Sam and Humphrey blossom as students in their respective interests: Sam works on his composing, and Humphrey is free to practice his piano playing without being exploited. The house emits a feeling of reassurance and relieves the bleakness of the boys' former lives, in contrast to the supernaturalism of the pesthouse in *Blackbriar* or the surrealism of the ghastly *House of Stairs*.

Sleator uses broad strokes to satirize such things as the Russian music critic's name—Nitpikskaya. The virtuoso, Prendelberg, and Tina, the publicity-seeking blond actress, are slapstick stereotypes. The fickleness of the concert audience is also parodied.

Reality and illusion are intriguingly intertwined. For example, Bridget uses real drugs to trick Humphrey into thinking he is being contacted by Magyar's ghost. The hands in the stained cloth also appear to be real, although they turn out to be from a doll. That all is not fully answered in the end should not bother us too much—many happenings in young people's lives must seem equally baffling to them.

Critical opinion on this book has been divided. The reviewer for the *Bulletin of the Center for Children's Books* liked it, saying, "For most of the dramatic and often funny story, the strangeness is explained, but there are occult elements (precognition) for one and there's some broad lampooning (the Russian music expert is named Alexandra Nitpikskaya) of types in the world of classical music. This has a lively pace, sharp characterization, good style, and often-acid humor."[1] Anita Wilson in the *School Library Journal* also praised it for the most part: "Sam is a well-rounded and sympathetic narrator who is convincing in both his lifelong jealousy of Humphrey and in his growing realization that he nonetheless cares for his brother and wants to protect him from exploitation. The characterization of Bridget is sometimes too exaggerated to be credible, but the book is highly suspenseful, with effective touches of horror, and should please young adult mystery fans."[2] William McBride in the *Voice of Youth Advocates* was not pleased, but how could he be when he was looking for another *House of Stairs? Fingers*, he says "is disappointing, partly because it is clearly not equal to *House of Stairs*. Then, too, the characters remain two-dimensional. The book may appeal to upper elementary or early junior high students, but it is not Sleator's best work."[3]

And most devastating to Sleator, Ann Durell, as we have seen, did not like it at all. Sleator says, "It made her feel unhappy because there is so much meanness in the book. And a lot of people who have talked to me about that book have said the same thing—that this book has a general feeling of bitterness and hostility that is a little bit unpleasant. The other problem is that the parents are the bad guys." But Sleator claims *Fingers* was intended as a farce: "I love that book. It has style. It was supposed to be funny. It is an exaggeration. Ann didn't get it."

Durell has rejected four other manuscripts of his—two sequels to *Into the Dream,* a book about an English ballet school, and a book about a werewolf in the 1930s. Sleator says, "I think Ann was right to reject those manuscripts, and they have remained on my shelf. *Fingers* was the one book rejected by Ann that I continued to believe in—partly because my mother thought it was so good. I am very thankful that Jean Karl at Atheneum wanted to publish it." Sleator likes the writing style, which he says he has never been able to repeat but hopes someday again to come up with lines like "peevish medieval plumbing, more often than not too dispirited to flush with adequate conviction."

Probably another reason Sleator likes this book is that it is the only one in which he writes about music and about what it is like to compose music. *Fingers* is also the first book Sleator wrote in the first person, a point of view he liked so much that every book he's written since uses it. He says the great challenge of the first person is to be indirect—to let the reader know things the first-person narrator does not know. He says he's still working on that.

Interstellar Pig

Although Sleator draws on a house he once lived in as the setting for *Interstellar Pig* (1984), with this book he is back to science fiction. He began writing it while staying one summer in a cinder-block cottage next door to a captain's house. He was trying to write a nautical yarn, and the effort turned into a science fiction story. Sleator says, "Maybe I am being influenced by some subliminal power from the stars. Try as I might, I can't seem to keep outer space, time travel, and aliens out of my work."[4]

The story is told by 16-year-old Barney, who is spending two

weeks with his parents at a New England beach resort called Indian Neck. Barney sunburns easily; evidently does not like to
swim; is bored, lonely, indecisive, and shy; and likes to read science fiction. He is living in the house belonging to a captain
whose brother was crazy and was kept locked in a room (Barney's
bedroom, as it turns out) for 20 years. Strange grooves are
scratched in the wall and window facings.

Three unusual individual move into the cinder-block cottage
next door. Right away Barney notices that his parents do not see
the three in the same way he does, or even agree between themselves on what they look like. The mother thinks the woman is
too old to wear a bikini and the men look like models. The father
thinks the woman is gorgeous and the men puny. Barney thinks
they all look great and are just a little older than he. They move
with an animal grace that makes Barney think he is watching
three lions. They appear to be foreigners by the way they speak
English.

The first time Barney visits their house, he sees Zena, Joe, and
Manny playing Interstellar Pig, a board game involving exotic alien creatures who are searching the universe for an object called
The Piggy. Intrigued, Barney wants to learn how to play the
game.

From the first, the three take a great interest in Barney, which
pleases his teenage need to put one over on his parents—these
exotic people like him best. They manage to get into his house
and comb through it the way archaeologists would. Since they
have searched his house, Barney feels it is only fair to search
their house while they are out. As he has in several other novels,
Sleator comments on the part chance plays in the course of life.
Barney says, "And now I wonder: How differently would things
have ended if I hadn't found what I did that day?"

In Zena's room he finds portions of the sea captain's diary (the
same one who owned Barney's house), telling about the murder
of a man picked up at sea. The captain's brother was the mur-
derer, and, to punish him, he was keelhauled, that is, dragged
from one end to the other under the boat. For a moment when the
captain first glimpsed the victim he saw a green reptilian crea-

ture with a sluglike thing in its mouth—but only for a moment. The captain took his by-now-brain-damaged brother home and locked him in a room until he died twenty years later. The brother had with him a trinket he had taken off the dead man's body and had clung to even while being keelhauled. That object is what the neighbors are searching for.

Zena teaches Barney to play Interstellar Pig while sitting in the blazing sun (deliberately to burn him, the reader finds out later). Barney innocently thinks, "My body was so white, compared to hers, that we could have been members of different species." Zena easily defeats Barney and gives him the rule book to take home to read on his own. The words on the page seem to crawl, until his eyes adjust and he can read what is written.

Barney soon figures out that the marks on the wall and window casing all point to one spot on a nearby island. He decides the trinket must be hidden there, and he is determined to get it first. The three neighbors are also planning a trip to the island by surfboarding. Joe, who Zena says is best at "aquatic" activities, is none too happy to take Barney with him but finally agrees. Barney had noticed earlier that the three have a purplish cast to their skin. Since he has to lie flat on the surfboard with his face at Joe's feet, he especially notices that Joe's toenails have purplish stains under them. Once the group reach the island Barney is able to find The Piggy, hidden in a trunk exactly where the lines scratched on his window had shown it would be. He is able to keep the others from finding out he has it, at least until he is safely back home.

Sleator gives enough hints so that the reader is able to figure out long before Barney does that these three are really alien creatures. Each of the three try to bribe Barney with incentives, such as extreme intelligence and life everlasting, in exchange for The Piggy. He refuses all offers and later thinks of a clever hiding place, the hollowed-out inside of a high school yearbook.

The aliens contrive to get Barney's parents away for the day and evening, leaving Barney to fight them off alone. As in several other Sleator novels, an adolescent manages to save the world even though it does not know it needs to be saved.

Zena suggests they play a game of Interstellar Pig, this time for real stakes. Barney realizes he is playing for keeps, if what Zena has told him is correct: that if he doesn't win, the earth will be destroyed. The Piggy also tells him that if he possesses it when the game is over, it, The Piggy, will hiccup and destroy the world.

At the beginning of the game Barney chooses several weapons, including a "Disguise Selector" and an immunity pill. Barney takes the immunity pill hoping it will be of some use. Not only are the three aliens after The Piggy, but so are other aliens who have thus far been only character cards. In the first game he played with Zena, Barney had been a lichen from the planet Mbridlengile. The lichen live in "colonies of hundreds or thousands of individual cells. . . . Each cell is capable of absorbing chemical data from its immediate surface and transmitting it to the rest of the colony. . . . The individual cells are incapable of passing on false information; they cannot 'lie' to one another. . . . They are capable of eating through almost any obstacle to their progress." As Barney waits for the attacks from Moyna (Manny), Zulma (Zena), and Jrlb (Joe), the lichen ooze under the kitchen door.

Once the lichen are in the house, to keep them in Barney cuts his finger and drips blood across the doorways and window sills, hoping the immunity pill he took earlier was still in his bloodstream. Knowing that the lichen eat almost anything, and wanting to keep them as a possible weapon to use against the others, Barney throws them a package of bologna still in its plastic. They love it. Not only is Barney worried about losing The Piggy and his own life, but he suddenly realizes his parents may come home and could be eaten by the lichen or killed by any one of the other three aliens.

Using the "Disguise Selector," Barney turns himself into a lichen to avoid being tortured by Moyna, Zulma, and Jrlb. Thanks to the immunity pill, Barney is ignored by the other lichen as they ooze over the floor devouring everything, including lots of tiny bugs: "It was like subsisting on endless trays of hors d'oeuvres."

Barney, the pseudolichen, discovers that The Piggy is just some sort of recording device whose aim is to get around the universe to find out about as many species as possible. The game was invented for that very purpose, and this is still the first game. Barney, deciding it would be less dangerous for the lichen to win The Piggy, is able to tell them where it is hidden and leads them to it. The fact that his immunity to them has probably worn off worries Barney. As the lichen are leaving the house, they try to get around Barney, who is trying to break away from them. Barney says, "I did the lichen equivalent of elbowing and kicking as they swarmed past me, cursing me, furious and uncomprehending." Using the "Disguise Selector," he turns himself back into Barney; unfortunately, however, the lichen, as they squeeze under the kitchen door with their prize, The Piggy, chew a hole in the top of each of Barney's big toenails. This makes the reader cringe along with Barney but also chuckle at the absurdity of it all.

As they blast away in their ships, the three aliens decide Barney is more stupid than they thought, because he did not kill them when he had a chance. They zoom away in pursuit of the lichen, who are on their way back to their planet with The Piggy. The game goes on. The messed-up house is Barney's only proof all these events were not a dream. His life will now return to normal—or will it? He has had several exciting days in the company of three highly unusual people who have almost treated him as an equal and who have involved him in life-and-death situations. He has been attracted to an exciting female, an experience that may result in a new interest in the females of his own species. Barney has become more aware and will face the future as a more confident young man.

Barney's parents seem oblivious of his activities. They have brought him to the beach for a vacation, knowing he is allergic to the sun. During the day they are on the beach and at night they watch TV. When his middle-aged, out-of-shape parents disagree on what the three neighbors look like, Barney thinks they are behaving childishly as they try to rationalize their way out of being compared unfavorably with the new arrivals. Barney is also surprised that they are so interested in finding out about neighbors who have no obvious social position. On the beach Barney sees his mother as a "greased corpse" among the others and escapes back to the "safe darkness of the house." When Joe is about to introduce Barney's parents to one of the most influential families in New England, his mother gushes so that Barney thinks she sounds like a 14-year-old. The parents are not much concerned about leaving their son to be entertained by the neighbors; instead they caution him not to make a pest of himself.

When Barney is faced with the knowledge that the three are aliens and he is in the real game of Interstellar Pig, he has no adult to turn to for help or advice. Rather, he is the responsible one who must try to save the earth, save himself, and protect his parents from the aliens. He alone is able to see the aliens for what they are, perhaps because he is a teenager. At least Manny thinks so. He says, "Maybe they're harder to put things over on than—." After Barney gets rid of the aliens, he whistles calmly as he goes about sweeping up all the dead lichen mixed with sand, matter-of-factly thinking, "It was always that way at the beach—no way to keep sand out." It is now safe for his parents to return home to their dinner and their TV.

The three aliens have distinct personalities. Zena is strong-willed and dominant. She seems to be the boss, forcing the other two to cooperate until The Piggy can be located. She has a spectacular figure, long black hair, a husky voice, lavender eyes, and a deep tan. She can be smiling and cajoling in one situation, be "massive, brusque, in control" in another, and have a "rapid, high-pitched, silly giggle, like a teenager's" in still another. She is really Zulma, an arachnoid nymph from Vavoosh who has a fat, spiderlike body with eight jointed legs, and a humanlike, female head with huge, faceted eyes. She is the most intelligent of the aliens and gets very angry when she does not win the board game of Interstellar Pig. She is ruthless and regrets not killing Barney when she had a chance.

Joe is tall and strong, has a brown mustache, likes to swim—especially at night—and only grudgingly accepts Barney into the group. He is the one who lures Barney's parents away with the promise of boating with the Powells, one of the socially elite families on this part of the coast. In actuality he is Jrlb, a water-breathing "gill man" from Thrilb who looks like a swordfish with rudimentary arms and legs. He has a lower intelligence than Zena. In the final game he ties up Barney and tortures him by cutting him with the three-foot-long sword on his head, until Zulma appears. Jrlb manages to step into a patch of lichen who eat a piece out of his foot before he escapes into hyperspace.

Manny, the third alien neighbor, has some female characteristics. He has a blond beard, is more slender than Joe but wiry, giggles, is squeamish about Joe's bashing baby octopuses, reads fantasy and science fiction, bleaches his beard, thinks Barney's book sounds "enchanting," admires Barney's kitchen, likes to cook, competes with Zena to get the best tan, is in a snit because his dinner may be overcooked, and won't open a bottle of champagne because corks make him nervous. He is the alien female Moyna, "one of the octopus gas bag creatures from Flaeioub." Moyna comes the closest to getting The Piggy. Barney does his best to protect her from the lichen, even though he has to turn himself into a lichen to escape being killed by her. Moyna throws cutlery to try to kill him, and almost manages it. The lichen do puncture Moyna's portable breathing bag, and she nearly suffocates from lack of hydrogen. To keep her from dying after the lichen leave, Barney carries her outside, which he says was "like carrying entrails." Reviving, she cuts his arm as she speeds off to her spaceship. In the epilogue she says she wished they had killed Barney and his parents and is disdainful of Barney because he saved her life.

Although most of the story does take place in the two houses near a beach in New England, the setting-within-the-setting is the game itself, Interstellar Pig. When the characters are playing, they are in space and seem to be actually on the various planets they land on. The equipment cards the players draw show a neural whip, oxygen-breathing equipment, the "Disguise Selector," an immunity pill, an automatic translating headset—but the most fantastic card of all is hyperspace, which enables its possessor to travel anywhere in the universe in a second. The Portable Access to the Fifth-dimensional Matrix is what allows Jrlb to appear and disappear so easily when attacked. On the board this access is represented by black funnels called hyperspace tunnels.

The final game is played in the captain's house, which becomes the game board.

The players reveal their real selves—"a hairy spider-lady; a fish-man with a long, razor-sharp horn growing out of his head; and a flying octopus with claws." This mix of the alien with the ordinary, one of the characteristics of Sleator's science fiction style, is most effective in the last half of the book.

All are defeated by a 16-year-old boy who makes use of his own ingenuity and a few of the alien weapons available to him. Even though he has the power to destroy the three aliens, he chooses not to, because he likes them and there is no reason to destroy them. He alone realizes that it is just a game and not to be taken seriously. He doubts the world will be destroyed or that The Piggy is telling the truth about its hiccup. But he is doubtful enough that he plays to win, and because of this doubt he is willing to let the lichen win The Piggy and take it off with them, never to return to planet Earth.

Even though Moyna, the "octopus gas bag," has an arsenal of alien weapons, she still resorts to throwing a broken cola bottle, a cast-iron frying pan, and a bread knife, before she uses her alien weapon, too late. This cartoonlike sequence is full of humor and no one is hurt by it. Later Barney has to clean up this mess in the kitchen because he thinks he would have a hard time explaining why the kitchen equipment is sticking into the walls.

Many reviewers of later works by Sleator compare them with *Interstellar Pig*, which most agree is one of his finest novels. As one reviewer puts it, "compelling on the first reading—but stellar on the second."[5] The *Booklist* reviewer says, "Sleator draws the reader in with intimations of danger and horror, but the climactic battle is more slapstick than horrific, and the victor's prize could scarcely be more ironic. Problematic as straight science fiction but great fun as a spoof on human-alien contact."[6] The book did not get that way easily, according to Ann Durell, who says that when the book came to her,

> there was very little in it that could be used. I think this book *Interstellar Pig* demonstrates the editorial dynamic between

Bill and me at its most mysterious. I didn't write extensive detailed editorial notes. I couldn't, because I wasn't saying "change this" or "change that" but rather, "this story (in some ways nonstory, as I recall!) doesn't work."

This book took several rewrites, and even then the book still lacked a device to propel and rationalize the plot. At that point in my life, I was spending a lot of time playing board games with my 11-year-old stepson, so—"How about making it a game?" I suggested. And that was the McGuffin!

Sleator mentions *Interstellar Pig* in two of his later novels. Omar and Laura play the Interstellar Pig game on the computer in *The Boy Who Could Reverse Himself.* And David and Angela are watching the movie *Interstellar Pig* at the end of *The Duplicate.*

Singularity

Sleator is again back to science fiction in *Singularity* (1985). The idea had been floating around in his head for several years. He says the book almost wrote itself, "partly because it's about time, an extremely peculiar phenomenon and therefore one of my favorite subjects. There was a kind of inevitability about it." He had "been wanting to write about a room or building that had the properties of the playhouse in this story—a place where the flow of time is distorted." But, he says, "I didn't know where it would be, or what kinds of characters would stumble on this place." When he began writing the book he wasn't thinking about gravity or black holes; he was simply writing about 16-year-old twin brothers who are house-sitting at an isolated farmhouse in Illinois. The book is dedicated to Sleator's sister, Vicky S. Wald, who some people thought was the author's twin. He says in the dedication, "We are just as important to each other as any twins I ever heard of."

As the story begins, the twins' mother's Uncle Ambrose has just died, leaving the house to her. Since their parents are going to a convention in San Francisco for two weeks, the twins offer to leave their home on the East Coast to go to Illinois to check on the house. Uncle Ambrose was the eccentric black sheep of the family, a man who had a glass eye and would take it out and show it when people asked. He "looked sixty when he was forty," an interesting bit of foreshadowing. Barry is eager to go and convinces his twin, Harry, that it would be fun to have just the two of them around for a while. Recently the twins have grown apart, and in the hope they can be close again, Harry agrees to go. Fred, their cocker-spaniel mutt, will go too because their mom believes he will act as a watchdog.

At the farm the boys discover just how eccentric Uncle Ambrose was. One of the rooms in the house is filled with mounted skeletons of strange animals, such as a cat with six legs and a snake with a bird's head. Most unusual, though, is a building that seems to be a playhouse, 12 feet long and 6 feet wide, with no windows and only one locked metal door, like that on a bomb shelter. The structure is supplied with survival rations, multivitamin capsules, water, and lots of books.

At the farm they meet Lucy Coolidge, who tells them of her grandfather's difficulties with Uncle Ambrose and of the prize animals that strayed onto his land and just disappeared. On the property was a big flat rock, called Skeleton Rock by the Indians because there were always animal skeletons around it. After a good milk cow aged 20 years in a few minutes near the rock, Uncle Ambrose built the playhouse over it, and no other animals were lost.

The three discover the playhouse is full of spiderwebs and the bodies of dead bugs. As they go inside they notice there is a rabbit in the yard, and Fred is going toward it. When they come out several minutes later both the rabbit and Fred are in the same position. Later Barry gets locked inside the playhouse for what to him is all day and night but to Harry on the outside is only seconds. When Fred is accidentally shut inside for a short while, only his skeleton is left when the boys get the door open. Time thus goes faster in the playhouse.

Sleator uses the scientific theory of black holes as the basis for his explanation of the speeding up of time. Black holes are collapsed stars with tremendous mass and relatively little volume: "Because of gravitational tidal forces there is a radius around a black hole known as the event horizon, in which time almost completely stops" ("SP"). Sleator thought it only logical that if time slowed down on one side of a black hole, then it must speed up on the opposite side "to preserve the conservation of momentum." And *singularity* is the scientific term for the core of a black hole. The singularity is the one-way tunnel through which alien objects (such as the six-legged cat) might be pulled. When Sleator learned about the term he knew he "had the perfect title with an ironic double meaning: 'Singularity' meaning the black hole, and 'Singularity' referring to twins who are not twins at the end of the book" ("SF"). Sleator takes us beyond an acceptance of the theoretical construct of the black hole; he allows his characters to see—in the reflections on the water in the playhouse sink—what is coming down the tunnel.

Although the twins are identical, Harry feels inferior to Barry and wishes he were not linked to him. Barry is directive and often mean to Harry; Harry is meek and doesn't retaliate—until, that is, Harry decides to sneak out while Barry is asleep and spend the night in the playhouse, so that he will be older than his brother and able to lord it over him. For Harry the night will be one year long. During that year he exercises, reads, listens to music, meditates, and watches some strange object—a huge mouth—come closer and closer in the sink, the opening of the singularity.

When he comes out the next morning, Harry is a year older and three inches taller. Unexpectedly, Barry is sad because he feels his brother is now dead. Harry's realization that his twin did not hate him is the turning point in their relationship.

Just after Harry leaves the playhouse, the thing that has been approaching for a year arrives with an explosion. Harry somehow knows he has to let it out of the playhouse: "Out reared the head, swinging back and forth—though it wasn't really a head, only a pair of metallic jaws about the size of a small stepladder. Laser-like red points gleamed from the ends of the black conical teeth. Behind the hinge, the jaws were attached to a snakelike body of interlocking cylinders the color of steel, about a foot in diameter where they joined the head. Whiplike, convulsive, the thing uncoiled from the door, the jaws pointed skyward, darting and circling."

The creature, which Harry later decides is a robot, bites its tail and continues doing so until it devours itself and there is nothing left. The granite slab the playhouse is built on has cracked, and through the open door the young people see birds and hear noises, unlike before. Now time is the same inside the playhouse as outside.

Harry believes the robot has been sent to close the singularity, to keep something dangerous to our world from coming through the one-way tunnel. As in many of his science fiction novels, Sleator implies there is intelligent life in space—in this case, one or more benevolent beings who are thinking of the welfare of the earth. Would other beings out there really be that benevolent? Would they really be so far advanced that they would understand time warps and space configurations to see and make use of them?

Sleator chose to set this novel in the Midwest after a visit to see his parents, who live on the Illinois prairie. Sleator says, "I've always been appalled by the way easterners think there is nothing in the middle of the country. And on this particular occasion, after being in Europe, I was struck by how strange and exotic the prairie really is, so I got the idea of putting easterners out there." He drove around small towns, taking notes and making crude sketches. He says, "It all just fell into place."

Sleator says that when he decided to write about twins, he contacted as many twins as he could to learn how they felt about each other. All reported they had no problems; everything was perfect. Those same people wrote him after reading *Singularity* to say that that was just what being a twin was like. Certainly sibling rivalry will no longer be quite so devastating to Harry.

The character of Harry progresses from a shy, insecure, dependent boy to a very confident older brother who will no longer allow his "twin" to make fun of him or order him around. He continues his exercise program in the real world and after his long confinement will not soon take such things for granted as sunlight, grass, and the songs of birds.

Barry is also a well-rounded character, one who pushes his brother a bit too far. Lucy has been attracted to Barry and has chosen to side with him against Harry. She is as interested as the boys are in the mystery of the playhouse. Her reaction to the "new" older, muscular, taller Harry indicates Barry has just lost his attraction for her. The parents, as they usually are in Sleator's novels, are incidental. Their function is to give the boys a reason for going to the house and to provide the first indications that Uncle Ambrose and his property may be out of the ordinary.

Although some questions are answered and problems resolved by the end of the book, other, important ones are left unanswered. For instance, what will be the reaction of the parents when they return? What will they think, and how will they accept no longer having twins? Readers have been shown the parents only briefly, at the story's beginning, and so they have only Harry's word that "if Barry can adjust to me, then [our parents] should be able to." It is a typical Sleator ending and appropriate to the novel.

Most of the reviews of this book were positive. Some felt it was weak in characterization, but most thought it a suspenseful story told by a master storyteller. David Gale in the *School Library Journal* said, "Sleator is remarkably able to explain the scientific complexities of his plot without impeding the narrative flow, and the story remains gripping through its stunning climax."[7]

Ann Durell says about this story: "*Singularity* was an easy one for me. I thought and still think it was some of Bill's finest writing, especially in the way he evokes the Midwest setting. The book required very little editing; in fact, I turned it over to another editor, as I was desperately pressed with administrative problems at that time."

Sleator himself says about the writing of this novel: "Even in the middle of the book, new bizarre ideas would pop up that suddenly became integral to the plot. I wish all books progressed so straightforwardly. And certainly my editor at Dutton, Julie Amper, was a tremendous help in the writing of this book."

6. Science Fiction for Older Adolescents: Becoming More Daring

With *The Boy Who Reversed Himself* (1986), *The Duplicate* (1988), and *Strange Attractors* (1990), Sleator sets a standard of maturity in science fiction. He is comfortable in these novels with the physical and mathematical absurdities of the universe, multiple dimensions of space, duplication, chaos, and time travel. Sexual attraction is a factor in all three plots, at least more so than in earlier works.

The Boy Who Reversed Himself

Sleator says, "I have always known about the fourth spatial dimension. It's as fascinating to me as time travel, but I didn't know I was going to end up describing it when I sat down to write this book. The fourth dimension just kept creeping in—and then swallowed up the whole story."[1] He says the fourth dimension figures in some of his favorite science fiction stories, such as "All Mimsy Were the Borogoves," by Lewis Padgett, and "And He Built a Crooked House," by Robert Heinlein. It still surprises Sleator that he didn't think of writing about it sooner: "As far as I know, this is the only novel in which half the action actually takes place in the fourth dimension, and again I did a lot of research and tried to be as mathematically accurate as possible." The idea of multiple dimensions of space and guardians at each level who protect the borders of their dimension from discovery is a complicated one. But it works, and it works rather well. As the reviewer in *Publishers Weekly* so aptly put it: "Once again, Sleator treats us to the best that YA science fiction can offer: average—and sometimes not-so-average—teenagers facing the physical and mathematical absurdities of our universe."[2]

As is always the case, Sleator uses typical adolescent characters in routine suburban lives at home and at school as his springboard to science fiction. Laura, the narrator, is in the tenth grade. She is tall, pretty, and smart, but she is also a snob who uses people to get what she wants. Laura has been the tallest girl in her class since junior high school and has never had a boyfriend.

One day she finds a note about a test, the note written in mirror image and taped to her locker door—a little unusual but not unbelievable. Of course, it is a hint of more unusual things to come. The note is from Omar, who is shorter than Laura, is overweight, has a right front tooth missing, and lisps. He also has a foreign accent and is not familiar with TV, cookies, or much of anything else. His explanation is that he was born in Switzerland and has just come to this country. A Swiss who wears sandals in winter? Where did he really come from?

Omar lives in an old stucco house where the shades are closed all the time and where thick, unkempt pine trees crowd against the windows. He lives here with Mr. Campanelli, a strange old foreigner who stays in seclusion except when emerging to protest the highway department's plans to tear down the block. Omar is an apprentice to Mr. Campanelli, who is one of the guardians to the second dimension. Omar is being groomed to replace the old man, but not before he learns to protect himself from those who will try to learn the power of dimensional travel to exploit it selfishly.

Laura has forgotten an important biology report at home. When she opens her locker, however, the report is lying on top of her books but is now written in mirror image. She quickly slams the locker shut before she realizes she has forgotten the combination.

Omar sends her off to class, promising to bring the report to her later. When he does so, Laura notices that although her report is now printed correctly, Omar's hair is parted on the opposite side and his missing tooth is now on his left side. Laura confronts Omar and gradually forces out of him information on the existence of the fourth dimension. This task is not too hard, since Omar is lonely, weak, and easily persuaded.

When Omar takes Laura into 4-space she thinks at first it is a nightmare world. There are slimy globs of flesh-growing eyes, cartilage, and mouth—separating, squirming, and fusing—as she sees them inside and out, in cross section and in parts. She is horrified but still wants to know all about everything, for she wants to use time travel for her own ends: obtaining answers to tests, spying on others, entertaining friends, and getting in free at rock concerts. She does not seem to be bothered by the fact that she is using Omar, or that she is interfering with other people's lives by moving through the dimensions. While in 4-space she gets reversed, which turns her whole world around. When she returns home she must cope with everything backward. She can't even eat, because food does not taste the same when the taste buds are reversed.

As she has manipulated Omar, so does her arrogant almost-boyfriend, Pete, manipulate her. Omar tries to tell her of the potentially terrible results of what she both is doing and wants to do, but Laura can't resist involving Pete, the boy she's wanted to attract all along. By accident she is forced to take Pete into 4-space, where they are imprisoned and terrorized by Gigigi and Ramoon, inhabitants of the fourth dimension who behave much like human beings. It may be impossible for Laura and Pete to get back without endangering the normal world of 3-space. Ramoon, the dominant male creature, gives Laura and Pete a pair of special trinocular glasses through which Laura comes to see the order and beauty of 4-space. Ramoon wants to force her to tell how to get to 3-space. Laura and Pete can hear what Ramoon and Gigigi are saying in their minds—by ESP. Ramoon throws Pete into a maze reminiscent of *House of Stairs*. Using the trinocular glasses, Laura is supposed to rescue Pete before a wild-pig-like creature gets him. When she in turn is put in the maze, only Omar's interference keeps her from being devoured by the animal; Pete is almost no help at all. Laura quickly sees that home "wouldn't be home anymore, ever again" if the 4-space beings were to discover 3-space: "The creatures from the dimension above would have absolute power." Pete, however, is quite willing to show Ramoon the way back to 3-space if he can find it. Through her own wits and with Omar's help, Laura and Pete get back to 3-space.

The last chapter sums up their whole future life together and ties up the loose ends. Laura is a surgeon who uses her ability to go into 4-space to save lives. She has long been married to Omar and is writing about their adventures in a top-secret notebook "to engrave these events on my own memory."

Where is 4-space? Probably someplace either above or around us, but not necessarily, since 4-space involves a space alteration and an extra dimension. When Laura and Omar step out of the three-dimensional world into 4-space, they can see inside each other's bodies—bones, brains, digestive system, and so on. In 2-space there are only two dimensions, as in 1-space there is only one.

By putting the material in a notebook Laura has betrayed the secret of the delicately balanced worlds of different dimensions. Though the notebook is to be burned, she wonders what might happen if it fell into the hands of a publisher. That, says Betsy Hearne, writing in the *Bulletin of the Center for Children's Books,* "sports a note of humor that contradicts the suggested seriousness of the situation and gives the reader a sense of being part of a game played by the author. Readers who enjoy Sleator's other books will recognize his affinity for games."[3]

Some of the descriptions are fanciful and often funny. The 5-space lady has "hyperspherical eyes enmeshed in a kind of gooey web made out of things like beef tongues." The guardian for the fourth dimension is a singing blob. Laura first notices this creature sitting and belching out notes to a made-up jingle in Mr.

Campanelli's kitchen. She sees a four-foot-thick mound of flesh that quivers and pulses, glistens with moisture, and has a rolling blue eye.

Laura learns how dangerous dimension hopping can be when she is captured by the evil Ramoon, who is power hungry and will stop at nothing to be able to rule or destroy the third dimension. She decides to stay in 4-space or die rather than tell her secret to Ramoon, an action that redeems her. She has shown herself to be superior in many ways all along. For instance, whereas Pete is easily misled by Ramoon, Laura sees the alien for what he really is. On the return home, when Pete makes Laura an outcast she says, "Not being popular was a trivial sacrifice to make considering the larger issues at stake."

Gigigi, the female 4-space creature, is also superior in may ways. She feels deeply and cares about the two human beings. She is considered ugly by Ramoon because her features are reversed; somehow she has been to 5-space and has been turned around. In the end, however, Ramoon becomes ugly when he too is reversed and Gigigi is returned to normal, owing to Laura's intervention in her behalf. The caring woman triumphs; the opportunistic man loses and is now at her mercy.

Friends are a much more powerful influence than adults in *The Boy Who Reversed Himself.* While in 4-space Laura and Pete scarcely mention their parents. Even after their return we never see the parents' reaction to their children's absence. The young people are in charge of their own destiny.

An important theme of this book is the deceptiveness of appearance. Pete is a good example: he is handsome and seems to be intelligent and charming, but underneath he is self-centered, exclusive, unfair, and single-mindedly stubborn. In the lunchroom he won't sit with Omar, an underling, and he criticizes Laura for doing so. More revealing, Pete is willing to show Ramoon where 3-space is just to get home. He is really not very smart, and Laura finally realizes that. When he returns from the trip he forgets about 4-space and tells everyone how peculiar Laura is, which ruins her school life. He appears strong but is in reality weak and vindictive.

On the outside Omar doesn't look nearly as good as Pete. He is fat, short, and ugly. But underneath he is far kinder and stronger. He is patient and self-sacrificing. This positive side of him is shown in his relation to Laura. He informs her that a biology pop quiz will be given and picks up her report from her house after she forgets it. He is patient with her failures, and even when she betrays him he helps her out of trouble in the fourth dimension, putting himself in real danger. An unlikely hero in appearance but a true one after all.

Musician that he is, Sleator often uses music in different ways in his works. Here he makes an interesting use of Engelbert Humperdinck's opera *Hänsel und Gretel*. Mr. Campanelli loves the opera, and it blares from his house. In many ways Pete and Laura are like Hansel and Gretel. They in effect also lose their way home, are locked in a cage, and almost starve. And like Hansel and Gretel, they escape and get home safely. Sleator comments, "I filled the book—I'm not sure why—with references to 'Hansel and Gretel.' There are quotes from the Humperdinck opera, scenes of a boy and girl trying to find their way home through a forest, and even being put into a cage and fed gingerbread by an old crone. No one ever remarks on these resemblances to the fairy tale, though I don't know why anyone should, since they have no significance that I'm aware of. I was just playing around."

Sleator again uses the setting-within-a-setting in this novel. There is the normal, ordinary world of home and school, and then there is the world of the fourth dimension. Omar takes Laura on her first trip into the fourth dimension from her own bedroom. She sees parts of her room she could not see before, including little bugs inside the light fixture. She can also see the bones and veins inside her hand; Omar's brain inside his skull; and the inside of her mother's head. This part of 4-space fascinates her, but the creatures who live there repel her.

Sleator's descriptions of where 4-space is, how 3-space looks from it, and how 2-space looks from 3-space are ingenious. As Laura and Pete are being carried home by one of the guardians, she observes, "We stood on the shore of a lake. Not a 3-space lake, with a flat surface. A 4-space lake, its surface spherical, domed,

glowing from within, tilting away from us, curving around in the
ana and *kata* directions. And so, too, did the shoreline curve,
undulating *ana* and *kata* to enclose this strange body of water—
except that it was not water. It was space. Our space. The three-
dimensional surface of hypersphere."

Laura grabs Omar as they are being dropped back into their
homes in 3-space and ends up in Mr. Campanelli's basement,
where 2-space exists: "2-space was big. And it wasn't a flat plane;
it seemed to be a bubble. We weren't really in a basement, but in
a cave that extended into dimness as far as I could see. The only
light came from the gleaming shape, like some huge dirigible,
that curved away into the distance. The 2-space universe was the
flat surface of this balloon—just as our universe is the three-
dimensional surface of a 4-space hypershape."

The inhabitants of 2-space are shaped like a fat capital B and
have two eyes, one on each edge of the rounded B. They have two
limbs coming out of the top and two out of the bottom, limbs that
can serve as legs or arms according to the way they are flipped.
They have a nose and one ear. The inhabitants of 4-space have
three eyes, three nostrils, and two pairs of arms. The 5-space
creature has a scarlet eye shaped like "a solid hypersphere, an
eye within an eye within an eye," and behind and above hangs "a
tuba-shaped organ, spreading out and opening into a yellow cav-
ern festooned with twisting corkscrews of moist tissue." Laura,
even with the aid of the trinocular glasses, cannot see the whole
being. Each being has to have features that fit the extra dimension. Of course, three eyes would be necessary in 4-space, since
human beings need two in 3-space.

Each dimension has its own guardians against those who would
disturb the dimension below it. Were any dimension to be dis-
turbed by the one above, all would fall and chaos would result. At
the end of the book the highway department is just about to take
over the Campanelli house, and Omar has appealed for help to
the higher-dimensional guardians. What will be the result of their
interference in a lower dimension? Will chaos result? Can 2-space
be saved?

Again in this novel as in all his other science fiction writings, Sleator takes a scientific theory and creatively works it into a story. Though some of the machinery creaks at times, that aspect does not bother many science fiction fans, or even many reviewers. Michael Cart in the *School Library Journal* says, "Sleator begins by creating fully realized, sympathetic three-dimensional characters whom readers are eager to follow into an alternative 'terra' and 'incognita' as they boggle the mind and inspire an almost Lovecraftian horror."[4] He further praises its verisimilitude and comprehensible mathematics, concluding, "The sum of these disparate parts is a novel that is viscerally exciting, mentally stimulating, and deeply satisfying" (Cart, 108).

It is not too surprising that Ann Durell at first had trouble with this book. She says it put her "nose back to the editorial grindstone." For someone who is not a science fiction enthusiast the complex dimensions are hard to grasp, and to retain once they have been grasped. "Just trying to understand the fourth dimension, even with Bill's gift of lucidity, was hard work," Durell recalls. "And we had to do one of our ESP turns on the second half of the book, in which Laura and Omar go into the fourth dimension. I told Bill that he had gotten too carried away by the characteristics of the dimension and needed to step back and create a logical and suspenseful plot. Which he did (obviously!) most successfully."

Sleator made some major changes:

> When I began revising it, I noticed that the only female character in the book was a grotesque fourth-dimensional witch. I didn't like the implications of that, and I also suspected that people might read some kind of unintended significance into it. So I decided to make the protagonist a female. I called Ann to ask her what she thought about that, and she said it was fine—and then added that if the character was female I would have to be careful with the phrasing of certain sentences about how the fourth dimension enables you to put things into other people's bodies. We both laughed—but I also made sure to be very careful about the phrasing.

About the dimension complexities, he says, "Adults often say to me, 'I enjoyed this book, but, of course, I didn't really understand the fourth dimension.' Kids never seem to have a problem understanding it."

The Duplicate

Reviewers welcomed *The Duplicate* with enthusiastic comments. Susan Harding in the *School Library Journal* said, "Sleator has done it again, writing an intense thriller, with horror building gradually, in which science fiction blends skillfully with reality. . . . Sure to satisfy Sleator's many fans and to win him some new ones."[5] Ann Flowers in the *Horn Book* admired its plot but noted weak characterization in her review: "The book reminds one of *Singularity, The Boy Who Reversed Himself,* and *Interstellar Pig* in the mind-boggling circularity of its plot. The story is more admirable for cleverness of plot than characterization . . . but the book is certainly a very good read and boasts a most unsettling last line."[6]

Indeed *The Duplicate* is a chilling look at what happens when an exact copy is made of oneself. Probably everyone has wished at one time or another, when life has got particularly complicated, to be two people.

Sleator begins the novel with a question: "What am I going to do about Angela?" Sixteen-year-old David has made a date to study math with Angela, the girl he has wanted desperately to date, on the very day he must attend his grandmother's birthday party. What is he going to do? To forget his difficulties he goes walking on the beach, hoping to at least find a bottle with a message inside it. Instead he finds that the storm has washed up a charred object that "looks like a combination postage scale and video camera" and is about the size of a portable TV. He watches as a gull explores the object, and suddenly there are two gulls where one had been. On further examination he finds the name Spee-Dee-Dupe printed on the object. David thinks it might be a top-secret device. If so, printing Spee-Dee-Dupe on it hardly seems a good way to keep a secret. "Or else it's an artifact of the future, or another planet or something," a notion that doesn't bother him at all. The fact that it is charred might indicate it arrived from outer space, or, of course, someone could have tried to destroy it by burning it.

Putting two and two together, David decides this may just be the answer to his problems. When he gets the object safely home he experiments by trying to duplicate first a pen and then money. It won't duplicate objects, he concludes. Finally he tries a fish from the fishbowl in his room. The fish duplicates itself. David doesn't need much more to be convinced of the machine's powers and doesn't worry about its safety—he proceeds to duplicate himself. But immediately there is a hitch: Duplicate A thinks he is the original David. Almost from the first moment, David does not trust the duplicate. The two are faced with the problem of clothing, who sleeps in which bed, who eats what meals, and, more to the point, who has to go to Grandmother's and who gets to go on the date with Angela. The duplicate wins the toss of a coin and goes off to see Angela, leaving a very unhappy David to visit Grandmother.

That David's father works at a genetic-engineering firm provides a touch of Sleator irony. (His mother is a greeting-card artist who works at home.) When asked if it is possible to clone a person, David's father says there is no known technology that can do that.

The logistics of getting in and out of the house, to school, to band practice, and most of all to see Angela are complicated. While David is at school the next day, the duplicate finds a hideout on the beach in an abandoned army watchtower from World War II, a place avoided by even the local teenagers, because years before a boy had been murdered there. The duplicate moves the Spee-Dee-Dupe there during the day. David is afraid of the tower and refuses to stay overnight in it. When they return home, the duplicate insists on going to school in David's stead the next day. To get even, David calls Angela and asks her to skip school and join him for a day on the beach and at the movies.

David notices that one of the fish in the fishbowl is behaving strangely and has developed black marks on its head and fin.

What do they mean? He is soon to find out. He goes to the tower early the next morning and while exploring on the second floor is almost killed by a piece of concrete block balanced above a door. He is sure the duplicate is trying to kill him.

After spending a pleasant day with Angela, which includes a kiss or two, David returns to the tower. The duplicate attacks him as soon as he arrives and hits him for stealing Angela away for the day. As a test David asks the duplicate to open the door that was booby-trapped, which he does willingly. Just in time David grabs him as the same piece of concrete falls again. Who had put it there? The duplicate seems to know, and says he will spend the night in the tower.

The next morning the duplicate convinces David *he* should go to school again, and David can hide on the beach. He does tell David he can wait, and the two of them will go to the tower after school. He seems afraid and timid, and David gets the feeling that the copy is feeling sorry for him. There is a black mark on the duplicate's neck and a triangle-shaped black mark on his hand. Apprehensively, David agrees to the plan.

David finds one of the fish dead, and the one with the black marks going crazy in the bowl, snapping its two rows of razor-sharp teeth. It tries to bite David's hand when he reaches in to pick up the dead fish.

When David gets to the tower he finds a drawing on the floor—a bifurcation chart—"a line about a foot long that splits into a fork. The right fork continues on for another foot: the left fork splits into two lines again after six inches." (Sleator uses the bifurcation chart again in *Strange Attractors,* but much more elaborately.)

Inside the room is another duplicate. It seems Duplicate A had bifurcated himself on Monday while David was at school. Whereas the first duplicate looks almost exactly like David and likes Angela as much as David does, "This one looks slightly different from both of them. His hair light blond and very curly, his face narrow and almost elfin, with large eyes and delicate features and absolutely flawless skin." Duplicate B hates Angela and admits he put the concrete block over the door, hoping it would fall on her. He is extremely violent and wants David to help him kill Duplicate A. David manages secretly to paint a black streak on his own neck and a huge triangle on his hand and tells Duplicate B he is dying, as they all will soon unless there's only one of them. Not too smart a story to tell a violent bifurcation: David ends up being knocked out and tied up, with smelly socks crammed into his mouth.

Curious, Angela appears on the scene and is almost raped by Duplicate B before Duplicate A comes to the rescue. The latter, however, is very close to death and not thinking too clearly. Duplicate B throws him off the tower to his death, and it is Angela's quick thinking that causes Duplicate B to lose his balance and fall off the tower to *his* death before he can kill David—leaving, of course, the original David and Angela to bury the two duplicates, to figure out what to do with the Spee-Dee-Dupe, and to engage in a few kisses now that she sees what an unusual young man he is.

As Susan Harding in the *School Library Journal* says, "The gadget that sets up the story never becomes the story—the focus is always on David" (Harding, 113). Once David has duplicated himself he loses interest in what should have been a fascinating machine with which to experiment. He accepts without question the fact that the object may be from another planet, and he aims it at himself with no qualms about what it might do to him. David is one of those people who often act before thinking, and he accepts invitations for times he is already engaged and in general lets people down. For the sake of the plot, Sleator is probably justified in making David more interested in how to solve the problem of being in two places at once. At least David does not try to make two Angelas.

Characteristically, Sleator ends the book with a teaser. David and Angela are watching the video of *Interstellar Pig,* kissing, and discussing the Spee-Dee-Dupe, which they have dumped at sea after taking (what they think are) adequate precautions to keep it from washing ashore. David begins to wonder if the machine might have recorded his genetic material and Duplicates A and B could be inside the machine still, "ready to come out if a certain button got pushed accidentally or otherwise. And what would the duplicates do if they did get out?" Angela distracts him with a kiss—"until the phone rings." Who could be calling—Duplicate A? Duplicate B? the builders of Spee-Dee-Dupe? What is in store for David? Only William Sleator knows, and perhaps someday he will tell.

The contrasts among the characters of the three Davids are interesting. The original David is a fairly typical 16-year-old, interested in girls (Angela in particular), his appearance (he wonders if the duplicate's body is better than his own), school (but right now only in relation to shared classes with Angela and talking to her between classes), and band (his only after-school activity). From the moment he duplicates himself the real David is full of doubts about his own identity and that of the duplicate. He doesn't trust anything Duplicate A does or says. He keeps thinking there are ulterior motives. And the reader is given just enough hints to distrust Duplicate A as well. David begins to wish he had never made the duplicate. He realizes it is not exactly like him—he would *never* poke a stick into a jellyfish. "And since he isn't a totally accurate copy of me, there will probably be other differences too—unexplained differences—that I won't be prepared for," he thinks. David even gets to the point of wishing the duplicate were dead.

Duplicate A looks very much like David and seems to think like David, but he hides things from him. He does not tell David everything about his date with Angela, omissions that later make David look stupid. He is more stubborn than David and braver; David would never have gone into the tower alone. Duplicate A is the one in control, as he says when he realizes David is afraid he might be forced to stay alone in the tower.

Duplicate B is quite different from the other two, both in looks and in disposition. He is cruel and enjoys inflicting pain. He forces Duplicate A to do what he wants and is able to capture and beat David easily. Unlike Duplicate A, he knows he is a duplicate and not the original. He hates Angela, tries to rape her, and threatens to kill her to keep Duplicate A from attacking him.

An interesting question here concerns David's personality.

Since Duplicate A is an exact copy of David and Duplicate B is a copy of Duplicate A, are all three personalities what David is really like? Perhaps David is the superego, the one who functions to reward and punish through a system of moral attitudes, conscience, and a sense of guilt. Duplicate A is the ego that functions both in the perception of and the adaption to reality. And Duplicate B is the id whose source of psychic energy derives from instinctual needs and drives. The savagery of his behavior toward Angela and his battle for survival by trying to kill the other two parts of himself bear this out. David thinks Duplicates A and B— the ego and the id—are gone, but are they? Can one be whole without the other two parts of the psyche? Sleator seems to think not. There *is* that ringing phone at the end.

Sleator's main characters do not take advantage of others, even when their own lives are at stake. Just as Barney in *Interstellar Pig* cannot allow Moyna to die or to kill Jrlb or Zulma, so too does David refuse to push Duplicate B to his death when he has the chance. The three aliens cannot understand such behavior, and neither can Duplicate B: "You can't really have any respect for someone like that, can you, Angie?" he asks her. "Someone who doesn't have the courage to make a move for his own survival, who just stands there? Someone that weak and gutless hardly deserves to survive, don't you think?"

Just as Tycho in *Green Futures* is being chased by an older self who is trying to murder him, so too is David being attacked by a clone of himself. If not for the interference of Duplicate A, who isn't nearly so bloodthirsty as Duplicate B, and of Angela, David by himself would have been killed—definitely a frightening thought. Sleator continues this bifurcation idea in *Strange Attractors,* in which a duplicate Eve Sylvan and Professor Sylvan are trying to murder the originals.

Chaos is the eventual result of bifurcation, and sure enough, as in the other two books, the final scenes of *The Duplicate* are as near to chaos as is possible while still having order restored—or is it restored? Remember the ringing telephone.

Angela is a believable character. She likes David, and at least two of him are different enough to keep her interested. Through appealing to her sexually rather than intellectually, Duplicate B is able to get her inside the tower, an action she refused to do with David, and even up to the bedroom and onto the bed. When Duplicate A interferes in the near-rape, Angela is still loyal to B. Given that David has straight, dark blond hair and B has curly, light blond hair, one wonders if Angela needs glasses. But she does choose the correct David to help in the end.

As in most of Sleator's fiction, parents are not important characters. David's are mere stick figures; however, they are there to provide stability and to complicate David's life but not to interfere with it.

In this book too there are two settings. First is the normal, everyday world of David's house, where he duplicates himself and must face the inevitable problems of food and clothing and of keeping his parents from finding out there are two of him. Second is the world of the beach. David likes to walk along the shore when he is troubled. He feels as though the beach belongs to him, at least until he finds the machine whose use jeopardizes it for him. The sea is the source of life on earth. The machine comes from the sea and can produce new life—not very lengthy life, but life nevertheless. It is also returned to the sea to disintegrate or perhaps to bring forth new life again in a never-ending cycle.

The tower on the beach is a dark, mysterious, dangerous place that has been off-limits to David. It is inside the tower that the life-and-death sequences of the book are carried out. This is where the three parts of one person do battle for survival.

There are no alien worlds or beings in this book, no time warps or alternate worlds. There is only the alien device through which an insecure teenager becomes a confident adult. It is a different David at the end from the one at the beginning, who hardly dared ask Angela for a date. He has come a long way in three weeks. He and Angela have become very close while working through the cleanup and disposal of the bodies and the Spee-Dee-Dupe. There is no doubt he has won the girl. He still questions the future, but with Angela's help he can face it.

Sleator says, "My brother Danny, a computer scientist, gave me the idea for this book. I thought it was a very funny idea. But when I sat down and brainstormed, trying to be completely logical about it, I came up with a book that was totally different from what I had first imagined. There are certain passages that still make me scream."[7]

Ann Durell, to whom the book is dedicated, has this to say about working with Sleator on this book: "The scientific device he used in *The Duplicate* was much more straightforward, but the complex way in which he developed it in the plot called for a sharp editorial eye to make sure he kept the three 'Davids' straight. Originally he changed the narrative viewpoint to each duplicate as it was created, but I found this confusing and felt it prevented a taut line of suspense. At my suggestion he changed to one viewpoint (the real David's) and made it, I think, a much better story. Otherwise, very little editing was needed."

Strange Attractors

Sleator says of *Strange Attractors,* "At periodic intervals, the urge to write about time travel begins to pull at me—and like a strange attractor, it is impossible to resist."[8] In this case, instead of a device dropped by alien beings, as in *The Green Futures of Tycho,* a professor has built a time machine. No longer egg-shaped, it is "like a clunky, old-fashioned calculator, with a display screen and a small array of keys."

Sleator says of the origin of this book, "I laughed when my brothers told me that there was an actual science of chaos—the idea seemed absurd. Then I looked into it, and became fascinated, and obsessed. I read books, I went to chaos conferences, I unsuccessfully tried to teach myself calculus to understand chaos better (regretting very much that I had dropped out of calculus as a high school senior). I had piles of material, pages and pages of notes. Eager to write, I hastily brainstormed the book, and turned out a 240-page draft."

In *Strange Attractors* Max becomes involved with two girls who both claim to be Eve Sylvan, daughter of Professor Sylvan, the author of a major paper on nonlinear temporal dynamics. Unwittingly Max has taken a time machine from a lab he visited. When he discovers what it is he doesn't want to give it back to either of the two pairs of Sylvans. When the book begins, Max has somehow lost a day (which we later learn has occurred because he was drugged by the real Professor Sylvan so that he could hide the time device, the phaser, in Max's jacket). Max is an only child, one whose father is a professor. His parents are only slightly concerned with his loss of memory. As typical Sleator parents, they seem to handle his comings and goings without too much interest or concern.

Max, who has been out of high school a week, is older than most of Sleator's protagonists. He understands nonlinear temporal dynamics and wants to believe in the scientific reality of time travel. He has the sort of mind that tries to follow "the motion of individual bubbles as they were swept along toward the waterfall, trying to see the water not as a solid mass, but as an intricate network of wildly crisscrossing pathways." When faced with a chaotic bifurcation graph of period doubling he is fascinated by it—"And suddenly I was struck by a strange sensation of hopelessness." He seems to be a part of that chaos and is both sickened and excited by it. He later tries to explain the feeling to Professor Sylvan: "It scared me. The chaotic veil seemed really horrible somehow, sickening—but also exciting. I felt kind of like . . . I was falling into it just now. As if the strange attractor that pulls the system into chaos was pulling me, too." This strange attraction is not only toward the chart depicting chaos but also toward the first Eve, who holds that attraction throughout the novel.

Chance plays a big part in this novel, as it does in so many of Sleator's books. As Max says near the end of the novel, "If I had never met the other Eve, and had had that taste of adventure, I wouldn't have compared things in this way. . . . Such a small thing, but such a tremendous difference in the end: Sensitive dependence on initial conditions, the first rule of chaos." If he had answered the phone that was ringing as he ran out of the house, he would never have met the first Eve at all.

As in most of Sleator's books, houses are of great significance. The Sylvans live in a starkly modern, sparse furnished, poured-concrete house: "Balconies sprouted from different levels. . . . A large balcony on the right side of the house was cantilevered out over a waterfall." At the end of the driveway a Jeep Cherokee is parked within an area outlined in white paint. It is from this area that the Sylvans make leaps into the past in their car. By fixing the exact spot, they are able to escape the possibility of reappearing inside some object and risking certain death.

The Sylvans want something from Max, but he doesn't know what. He is very much attracted by Eve's beauty. She is as tall as he and holds her head as a dancer does; her eyes are gray and are outlined with dark make-up; she has prominent cheekbones and a small nose. Yet "it was her mouth that gave the arresting quality to her face. Her lower lip was full, her upper lip thin and sculptured, the shape emphasized by red lipstick." She has short, streaked, curly blond hair. She moves as smoothly as a cat and seems to be attracted to Max. As he leaves he just wants to turn around and go back to her.

On his return home, another Eve Sylvan calls and asks him to come over. This time the Sylvans live in a third-floor apartment that is quite different from the stark simplicity of the other Sylvan home. The living room is crowded with objects and furniture: "There were a couple of old couches, and fat, comfortable-looking chairs with lamps on little tables next to them. Edges of faded oriental rugs peeked out from underneath the furniture. Bookcases lined the walls, and magazines were piled high on the tables beside various clocks and figurines." Because Max thinks it would take a long time to accumulate all these things, he concludes they have to be the real Sylvans.

The first Sylvans's hideout in the past is on the exact same spot as the basement of this apartment building, enabling them to keep tabs on their counterparts and making time travel less dangerous for them. In Sleator's earlier time-travel book, *The Green Futures of Tycho,* the title character had many close scrapes as he moved through time from the bathroom of his home—startling his sister in the tub in one leap, his father shaving or his own self showering in another. No such narrow escapes are allowed in this novel, and great care is taken to keep the time travelers safe and separated from their own future or past selves. Max has a close call or two before he gets the hang of time travel,but not nearly so many as Tycho did.

The Eve in this apartment seems to be the same girl as the first one he met, but there are differences. She is shorter, more relaxed, and is wearing a loose dress. She wears no makeup, and her long, darkish blond hair is in a thick braid. This Eve slumps, and is softer, fleshier, quieter, and steadier than the other one. Max is not attracted to this Eve at all. He believes her when she tells him to be careful, but the moment he gets into his car he forgets about her and begins to think about the other Eve. The strange attraction has him firmly in hand.

The two Professor Sylvans, although the same person, also have their differences. The first Sylvan has red hair in a crew cut and a firm, youthful body. He is handsome, enthusiastic, and charming, but he can be aggressive and cruel when he doesn't get what he wants. He smokes cigarettes, uses various drugs—alcohol, marijuana, and opium. He doesn't watch his diet, because he can always go into the future and get a new heart and lungs, and liposuction does wonders for the stomach.

In contrast the other Professor Sylvan has long, unkempt red hair, a protruding stomach, and a slightly dazed expression. He is timid, has wrinkles, is a little jowly, and is certainly no athlete. This Sylvan and Eve "seemed to eat nothing but health food, yet they looked much less healthy than the others, who indulged in so many vices."

These two real Sylvans will not tell Max anything about the phaser, trying to keep him out of the whole mess. Max, however, is involved and refuses to be shut out. He has already retrieved the phaser from his jacket at the cleaners, but he somehow can't bring himself to give it up. Just as Tycho could not let the egg go once he had used it, so too for Max is there some strange attraction to the phaser, as there is with everyone who possesses it— except for the fake Eve, who is able to put it down with no qualms.

As it turns out, the real Professor and Eve had "sent something into the past, and suddenly another universe existed, with another Sylvan and another phaser. And that Sylvan made more bifurcations . . . timelines doubling and sprouting, rushing faster and faster out of control. . . . And at the end, the infinite jungle of chaos." This situation is reminiscent of *The Duplicate*. After David makes Duplicate A, Duplicate A then makes Duplicate B, and chaos is the result.

The new Sylvan and Eve had used the phaser to go into the future in that universe and had interfered to the point that universe was in chaos. They had escaped to the prehistoric past, where they could safely exist with no harm to the future. From this base they had invaded the world of the original Sylvan and Eve; now they want to eradicate them so that they can take their places. The false Sylvan promises Max there will be no more time travel once the other two have been eradicated. Threatening Max with death by sending him to the remote past—when the earth was molten—the false Sylvan gets him to register the biochemical makeup of the real Eve and Sylvan by touching them with his phaser. To do this Max travels a few hours into the past from the bathroom of the Sylvans' apartment. Max records first Eve and her teddy bear while she sleeps and then Sylvan dozing at his desk.

The false Eve truly seems to have fallen in love with Max and is extremely upset when her father sends not only the other Eve and Sylvan but also Max into the chaos of their old universe. When Sylvan takes the phaser away from Max, he screams. The connection with the phaser is a physical as well as a mental one.

Since Max is sent into chaos from the prehistoric hideout that is on the exact spot as the Sylvan's apartment house, he finds himself in the basement. His search for the Sylvans' apartment is reminiscent of Tycho's final quest through the house to find the closet where the egg/time machine is hidden. Max finally reaches the Sylvans, who are none too happy to see him until they discover that when he touched Eve he also touched the teddy bear. Luckily, there is another phaser hidden in the bear. Max leads the Sylvans to the basement, where they send themselves back to the prehistoric past. Sylvan is afraid to use the phaser and does so only because he must. Max has to push the ACTIVATE button himself to send all three into the past. Max and the Sylvans have traveled to an earlier time than that visited by the false Sylvans. Suddenly, Max is transported to the hideout. The false Eve had used the phaser to send her own father to his death in the molten earth past, and then had sought out Max: "It was horrible, Max. . . . But I had to. Everything changed when I saw what he did to you, when I saw how he'd been lying to me all along." Max is happy to see her and comforts her, but when the other Eve and Sylvan appear, the false Eve wants Max to kill them. Instead, Max uses the phaser on her.

He and the Sylvans return to the present, where the Professor disarms the phasers: "He dismantled them slowly and carefully, piece by piece. I watched in barely controlled agony, as though I were observing someone dissecting my own limbs. I could feel it throughout my entire nervous system when each phaser ceased to function."

Max is assured of a job with Sylvan and a bright future as a scientist. Eve too is going to turn out to be a distinguished scientist. She seems to have a special intuition about time travel. Max talks his problems over with her, but not his ideas for the future concerning the false Eve and the phaser.

But what about the other Eve, that strange attractor who so fascinated Max? He reveals that instead of sending her to her death he has simply sent her a couple of weeks into the future. She is still at the hideout, where he plans to visit her just as soon as he gets his phaser built. He reasons to himself, "I just need to talk to her, to explain, to see her one more time. It wouldn't be enough of a change to bring on chaos. I know I'm right about that. I have to be."

It is interesting to speculate why Sleator called the girls Eve. Here we have one Eve in prehistoric times, with Max getting ready to go visit her. Though he is not named Adam, could this Eve and Max begin a new race in a different past? The word *sylvan* means "of the woods or forest." Eve Sylvan is living in a wilderness at the end of the book, no doubt waiting for her Adam to come along.

Male-female relationships have gradually evolved in Sleator's works. Although some attention is paid to it in *House of Stairs,*

sex is not an essential part of the plot. Zena uses her sexual at-
tractiveness in *Interstellar Pig* to get Barney to tell her what she
wants to know. In *Singularity* Harry is jealous of Barry because
he is able to interest Lucy; one of the reasons Harry decides to
stay in the playhouse is that by becoming older he will be more
attractive to her. The male-female relationship in *The Boy Who
Reversed Himself* is one of friendship, though Laura and Omar
eventually marry. In *The Duplicate,* David does have a girlfriend,
and there is an attempted rape by one of the duplicates. After the
duplicates are gone, David and Angela engage in lots of hugging
and kissing; still, that seems to be the extent of it. But in *Strange
Attractors* there is finally a sexual relationship—between Max
and the false Eve—although it is not described in detail. This
strange attractor, sex, keeps drawing Max back to Eve, even at
the risk of changing the time line, which may ultimately lead to
chaos.

There are no alien worlds in this book, although there are visits
to the past. A scary, dark, almost-evil journey to 1910 Bangkok
ends in Sylvan's fake rescue of a phaser and the deaths of two
men. The chaotic world of a possible future is not an alien world
but our own earth. Max lands there in the same apartment building as the real Sylvans live in at the present. It is a frightening,
but not an alien, world, and it is peopled by human beings.

Unlike Tycho, who found that each change in the past caused
frightful repercussions in the future and so decided to destroy the
time-travel device, Max is unwilling to accept the situation when
the phasers are destroyed. He is going to build another one, and
he is confident he can avoid changing the past. This overconfi-
dence and the actions of the other Eve may indeed change the
future.

Max's parents are there but are of no consequence. They answer
the phone for him and give him the car but are only incidental.
The false Sylvan is not much of a father figure either. He forces
Max to do things against his will, urges him to drink alcohol, and
doesn't mind Max making love to his daughter. Instead, he en-
courages it so that Max will do as he says. His own daughter mur-
ders him because he has got rid of her boyfriend. The real Eve

and Sylvan have a better father-daughter relationship. But because she is the one who bosses him around and tells him what to do, it is not a normal pattern. He treats Max well, even hiring him to work with Eve and himself. The real Eve is more like a sister to Max and her father. There's no mention of Max's own parents at the end, and the reader really doesn't expect to read more about them; they have faded into the background where all good parents are to be, while the teenagers go on about their lives.

The first draft of *Strange Attractors* needed substantial editing, according to Ann Durell. She says, "I called Bill after I read the first draft, and told him I liked the first page! But I also told him all the elements were there for a marvelous book—now that he had set them forth by writing out this chaotic picture of chaos, he could take them and make a story. A marvelously intricate but absolutely clear and riveting one, as it turned out—the kind only Bill can write."

Sleator says, "She was right. I was so carried away with the material that I had dumped all my research into this manuscript, everything I knew about chaos, and it was too much for one book. I had also forgotten one of the most important rules for writing any kind of fantasy or science fiction—contrast. If everything is crazy and unreal, very soon none of it will have any impact, or any credibility. The reader has to have a firm grip on reality, something he can identify with or relate to; without that, the book will be a dreamlike mess."

The only problem they had was with the ending. Ann wanted Max to forget about the impostor Eve, because he realizes she is evil. But Sleator didn't want things to be so easy. He wanted the impostor to continue to prey on Max's mind—as he believed would happen in real life—and to end the book on a sudden note of ambiguity and suspense: Max has got to see her one more time, even if doing so brings on chaos. Sleator felt very strongly about this point, and Durell backed down.

Thus far, reviewers have agreed with Ann Durell's opinion that the book is "riveting." Cathi Mac Rae in the *Wilson Library Bulletin* called it a "ground-breaking novel of infinite perplexity" and clearly indicated Sleator was writing mature science fiction for older adolescents in his analysis of the time-travel concept—"a complex achievement within his trademark action packed science fiction format. Leaping from one cliff-hanger to another, teenaged Max's first-person account entices YA readers to follow his time travel logic puzzle, with an added dash of romance. Sleator's awareness of which story elements are teens' "Strange Attractors" has never been more evident, nor has his control been more skillful."[9] Mary M. Burns concludes her review in *Horn Book* as follows: "The two Eves, quintessential temptresses, are well named—one appealing to reason, the other to sensation—with the phaser as the forbidden fruit. Fascinating and believable, *Strange Attractors* will not disappoint Sleator fans."[10] And Michael Cart in the *School Library Journal* says, "Sleator's marriage of chaos theory and the convention of time travel is an ingenious literary conceit beautifully executed and—in the scenes of time travel and of a future world in chaos—brilliantly imagined." Cart concludes that the book is one of Sleator's "strangest and most attractive novels."[11]

7. The Future:
Away from Science Fiction?

Orson Scott Card says, "Five, ten, fifteen years from now we're going to have an astonishing number of hot young writers in the field to whom the name 'William Sleator' will be spoken with the same affection that many of us used to reserve for 'Robert Heinlein' or 'Andre Norton.'"[1] Card believes this will be so because of Sleator's narrative style, which is "honed to a fine edge, so that nothing is included that isn't an integral part of the story" (Card, 6). Moreover, Sleator's characters are compellingly drawn and he explains complicated science with simplicity and clarity while at the same time managing not to "write down" to his audience.

Sleator is still young, as writers go, and it is tempting to speculate what else he might do. He could compose and play much more music. He is very talented at that, and it has been an important part of his life since childhood. Sleator composed his first ballet for the Boston Ballet Company in 1975, at the request of Ron Cunningham, then the resident choreographer. He has written a number of notable pieces for the ballet since. The concept of his first ballet was Cunningham's idea—called *Saturday Morning,* the ballet was about women's liberation, told in the context of Saturday-morning cartoons. It ended with a battle between Wonder Woman and Superman. Sleator found writing the music fun, and composing this ballet was the only time in his life when something happened that might be called "inspiration": "One morning I was working on the men's dance, a kind of delicate gavotte. I sat down at the piano, and four hours later I looked at the music I had written, and had no idea where it had come from. I had no memory of those four hours. It was as though the music had been fed to me unconsciously—it was brutally joyous music, some of the best music I had ever written."

The following year (1976) Cunningham asked him to collaborate on a ballet based loosely on D. H. Lawrence's "The Fox." They called it *Incident at Blackbriar,* not because it had anything to do with Sleator's book but because they simply liked the sound of the name. Sleator says, "I scored it for flute, oboe, accordion, piano, cello, percussion, and the hammered dulcimer. The dulcimer and accordion together were an especially interesting sound. The seduction dance is in a strange $\frac{5}{4}$ meter, and one of the most exciting pieces I've ever written." That quotation makes it sound as if composing ballet music might be an important part of Sleator's future, but he is frustrated by the "note-by-note" struggle. And besides, the constant decision making of musical composition bothers him because, as he says, "I have always hated making decisions."

Sleator might do some reviewing, although his undergraduate experience on the Harvard *Crimson* does not seem to make that too likely. His mother had always thought one way he could have a secure job was as a critic, but applying for a place on the prestigious student newspaper was a grueling process. He had to write a review a week, none of which were published and all of which were scrutinized by an upperclassman already on the *Crimson.* A young woman who believed in Sleator's potential became his mentor, and after a semester of tryouts he was finally voted onto the staff.

At that time the *Crimson* had a comment book in which it pasted published articles on one page and staff comments on the opposite page. Sleator's first review got "absolutely blasted, torn apart, nastily and publicly ridiculed, since everyone read the comment book. I was so humiliated by this that I never wrote another review for the paper (though my name remained on the masthead). In fact, I couldn't bear to enter the *Crimson* building after that, or even walk past it—I would cross to the other side of the street." Since then, although he seems to have the ability, Sleator has refrained from writing criticism.

Sleator may choose to write more short stories, such as "The Elevator," a piece he recently wrote for Jane Yolen and Martin Greenberg for a collection of original short stories entitled *Things That Go Bump in the Night*.[2] In that story 12-year-old Martin lives with his father on the seventeenth floor of an old apartment building that has a small elevator. This elevator scares Martin, who tries to walk the 17 flights of stairs but is also afraid of the stairways. He is even more frightened of a fat lady who gets on the elevator a couple of times with him. To avoid her he runs down the stairs and breaks his leg. He is now forced to use the elevator. His father makes fun of his fears, leaving him in the elevator alone to face the fat lady, who gets on at the tenth floor: "'Hello, Martin,' she said, and laughed, and pushed the Stop button"—another Sleator ambiguous ending. This work indicates Sleator needs more room than the short story provides to develop his characters; remember, he stopped writing texts for children's picture books for that reason.

It wouldn't be surprising to see Sleator write something with Boston as the setting. He chooses to live there because he can do almost everything on foot, and he likes walking because it provides a better opportunity to see the "wonderful architecture in Boston." Sometimes he waxes lyrical about Boston when he says he is "always looking at beautiful things." He calls living in Boston "a privilege." Besides, he hates to drive.

Sleator loves to travel in other ways, those not involving driving. And he likes to write about his travels. He has a manuscript about his trips to Bangkok that may someday appear in print.

Of course, that "next book," whatever it may be, will come, but Sleator doesn't like to talk much about it. When he is working he says he is writing "for Ann Durell only." At times he has made what he considers a mistake in showing someone a book in progress. What happens is that "unless that friend tells me it is completely wonderful, the best thing I've ever done (which never happens), I get discouraged—and that can interfere with the work." Of that next book Sleator says:

> I probably shouldn't say anything about the book I'm writing on now. I'm a little superstitious, and I'm afraid that if I make predictions they won't come true. What I will say is that I'm trying to get away from science fiction for a while. I've written too many books recently about a kid finding a piece of technology which gives him fantastic, but limited, powers. I don't want to fall into a pattern, or a formula—even if it's a formula that readers like, and that sells books. So I'm trying something different. This one has no science and no technology in it; it really is mainly about personal relations. All I will say about it is that finally I'm using a lot of material about Thailand. I hope it will turn into something I can sell—but it's still too early for me to be sure about it.

It is hard to believe that the next book won't be science fiction or fantasy, but Sleator has veered away from them before and might surprise us. Sleator without science fiction at all in his future would seem to be the "nuttiest paradox" of all.

Notes and References

Preface

1. *The Green Futures of Tycho* (New York: E. P. Dutton, 1981), dust jacket.
2. Jim Roginski, *Behind the Covers* (Littleton, Colo.: Libraries Unlimited, 1985), 202; hereafter cited in the text.
3. "What Is It about Science Fiction?" *ALAN Review* 15, no. 2 (Winter 1988); 4; hereafter cited in the text as "SF."
4. "Getting to Be a Writer," pamphlet (New York: E. P. Dutton, n.d.); hereafter cited in the text as "GW."

1. William Sleator: Ahead of Time from Birth

1. Blair Lent, "How *The Sun and the Moon* Got into Film," *Horn Book*, December 1971, 590.

2. Works for Children: Sleator Novels in Miniature

1. Ethna Sheehan, review of *The Angry Moon, America*, 5 December 1970, 495.
2. Elizabeth Minot Graves, review of *The Angry Moon, Commonweal,* 20 November 1970, 199.
3. Betsy Hearne, review of *Among the Dolls, Booklist,* 1 January 1976, 628.

3. Young Adult Mysteries: Place and Plot Predominate

1. Margaret L. Daggett, "Recommended: William Sleator," *English Journal,* March 1987, 93.
2. Review of *Blackbriar, Publishers Weekly,* 26 September 1986, 91.

3. Review of *Blackbriar, Library Journal,* 15 May 1972, 1928.

4. Review of *Blackbriar, Publishers Weekly,* 17 July 1972, 122.

5. Linda R. Silver, Review of *Run, Library Journal,* 15 November 1973, 3457.

4. Science Fiction for Younger Adults: Experimenting with Nutty Paradoxes

1. Pamela D. Pollack, review of *House of Stairs, Library Journal,* 15 March 1974, 904.

2. Review of *House of Stairs, Library Journal,* 15 December 1974, 3248.

3. Review of *House of Stairs, Publishers Weekly,* 6 May 1974, 68.

4. Kathleen R. Roedder, review of *Into the Dream, Childhood Education,* April/May 1980, 306.

5. Review of *Into the Dream, Reading Teacher,* October 1980, 53.

6. Barbara Elleman, review of *Into the Dream, Booklist,* 15 February 1979, 936.

7. Pamela D. Pollack, review of *Into the Dream, School Library Journal,* January 1979, 57.

8. Ruth M. Stein, review of *Into the Dream, Language Arts,* February 1980, 189.

9. Review of *Into the Dream, Reading Teacher,* October 1980, 53.

10. Sally Holmes Holtze, ed., *Junior Authors and Illustrators* (New York: H. W. Wilson, 1983), 296.

11. Pamela D. Pollack, review of *The Green Futures of Tycho, School Library Journal,* April 1981, 133.

12. Neil Philip, review in *Times Educational Supplement,* 18 November 1988, 26.

5. In and out of Science Fiction

1. Review of *Fingers, Bulletin of the Center for Children's Books,* December 1983, 78.

2. Anita Wilson, review of *Fingers, School Library Journal,* October 1983, 173.

3. William McBride, review of *Fingers, Voice of Youth Advocates,* April 1984, 35.

4. *Interstellar Pig* (New York: E. P. Dutton, 1984), dust jacket.

5. Trev Jones, review of *Interstellar Pig, School Library Journal,* September 1984, 134.

6. Sally Estes, review of *Interstellar Pig, Booklist,* 1 June 1984, 1392.

7. David Gale, review of *Singularity, School Library Journal,* August 1985, 82.

6. Science Fiction for Older Adolescents: Becoming More Daring

1. *The Boy Who Reversed Himself* (New York: E. P. Dutton, 1986), dust jacket.

2. Review of *The Boy Who Reversed Himself, Publishers Weekly,* 21 November 1986, 76.

3. Betsy Hearne, review of *The Boy Who Reversed Himself, Bulletin of the Center for Children's Books,* January 1987, 98.

4. Michael Cart, review of *The Boy Who Reversed Himself, School Library Journal,* November 1986, 108; hereafter cited in the text.

5. Susan Harding, review of *The Duplicate, School Library Journal,* April 1988, 113; hereafter cited in the text.

6. Ann Flowers, review of *The Duplicate, Horn Book,* May 1988, 362.

7. *The Duplicate* (New York: E. P. Dutton, 1988), dust jacket.

8. *Strange Attractors* (New York: E. P. Dutton, 1990) dust jacket.

9. Cathi MacRae, review of *Strange Attractors, Wilson Library Bulletin,* November 1989, 97.

10. Mary M. Burns, review of *Strange Attractors, Horn Book,* March/April 1990, 210.

11. Michael Cart, review of *Strange Attractors, School Library Journal,* December 1989, 120.

7. The Future: Away from Science Fiction?

1. Orson Scott Card, "Books to Look For," *Fantasy and Science Fiction,* August 1988, 37; hereafter cited in the text.

2. "The Elevator," in *Things That Go Bump in the Night* ed. Jane Yolen and Martin H. Greenberg (New York: Harper & Row, 1989), 12.

Selected Bibliography

Primary Works

Novels

Among the Dolls. New York: E. P. Dutton, 1974.
The Angry Moon. Boston: Atlantic/Little, Brown, 1970.
Blackbriar. New York: E. P. Dutton, 1972.
The Boy Who Reversed Himself. New York: E. P. Dutton, 1986.
The Duplicate. New York: E. P. Dutton, 1988.
Fingers. New York: Atheneum, 1983.
The Green Futures of Tycho. New York: E. P. Dutton, 1981.
House of Stairs. New York: E. P. Dutton, 1974.
Interstellar Pig. New York: E. P. Dutton, 1984.
Into the Dream. New York: E. P. Dutton, 1979.
Once, Said Darlene. New York: E. P. Dutton, 1979.
Run. New York: E. P. Dutton, 1973.
Singularity. New York: E. P. Dutton, 1985.
Strange Attractors. New York: E. P. Dutton, 1990.
That's Silly. New York: E. P. Dutton, 1981.

Short Story

"The Elevator." In *Things That Go Bump in the Night,* edited by Jane Yolen and Martin H. Greenberg. New York: Harper & Row, 1989.

Nonfiction

"Getting to Be a Writer." E. P. Dutton brochure, n.d.
"What Is It about Science Fiction?" *ALAN Review* 15, no. 2 (Winter 1988): 4–6.

Take Charge: A Personal Guide to Behavior Modification (with William H. Redd) New York: Random House, 1976.

Secondary Works

Books

Beach, Barbara, ed. *Book Review Index*. Detroit, Mich.: Gale Research, 1987.

Commire, Anne. *Something about the Author*. Vol. 3. Detroit, Mich.: Gale Research, 1980.

Emory, Ann, ed. *Contemporary Authors*. Vol. 29. Detroit, Mich.: Gale Research, 1978.

Holtz, Sally Holmes, ed. *Fifth Book of Junior Authors and Illustrators*. New York: H. W. Wilson, 1983.

Mooney, Martha T., and Barbara Jo Rixiello, eds. *Book Review Digest (1987)*. Vol. 82. New York: H. W. Wilson, 1987.

Reginald, R. *Contemporary Science Fiction Authors II*. Detroit, Mich.: Gale Research, 1970.

Roginski, Jim. *Behind the Covers*. Littleton, Colo.: Libraries Unlimited, 1985.

Articles

Card, Orson Scott. "Books to Look For." *Fantasy and Science Fiction,* August 1988, 37–39.

Daggett, Margaret. "Recommended: William Sleator." *English Journal,* March 1987, 93–94.

Davis, James E., and Hazel K. Davis. "Another Author Study: William Sleator," *FOCUS* 15, no. 2 (Spring 1989): 26–29.

———. "Nudging Readers over the Edge into Science Fiction and Fantasy: William Sleator's Works." *Western Ohio Journal* (1989): 97–101.

Lent, Blair. "How *The Sun and the Moon* Got into a Film." *Horn Book,* December 1971, 589–96.

Book Reviews

Among the Dolls
Bulletin of the Center for Children's Books, March 1976, 118.
Hearne, Betsy. *Booklist,* 1 January 1976, 628.
Heins, Ethel L. *Horn Book,* February 1976, 53.
Kirkus Reviews, 15 October 1975, 1186.
Moline, Ruth E. *Language Arts,* February 1976, 200.
Publishers Weekly, 20 October 1975, 74.
School Library Journal, December 1975, 55.

The Angry Moon
Agree, Rose H. *Instructor,* April 1971, 132.
Booklist, 1 February 1971, 453.
————. 1 April 1971, 661.
Bulletin of the Center for Children's Books, May 1971, 145.
Catholic Library World, April 1971, 520.
Crossley, Winnifred Moffett. *Top of the News,* April 1972, 298.
Graves, Elizabeth Minot. *Commonweal,* 20 November 1970, 199.
Hanley, Karen Stang. *Booklist,* 15 April 1985, 1204.
Heins, Ethel L. *Horn Book,* February 1971, 48.
Library Journal, 15 February 1971, 718.
Publishers Weekly, 23 November 1970, 39.
Sheehan, Ethna. *America,* 5 December 1970, 495.

Blackbriar
Best Sellers, 15 August 1972, 244.
Booklist, 1 September 1972, 45.
Bulletin of the Center for Children's Books, October 1972, 31.
Daggett, Margaret L. *English Journal,* March 1987, 93.
Fantasy Review, December 1986, 41.
Heins, Paul. *Horn Book,* August 1972, 378.
Kellman, Amy. *Teacher,* October 1972, 115.
Kirkus Reviews, 15 April 1972, 486.
————. 15 December 1972, 1421.
Library Journal, 15 May 1972, 1928.
Publishers Weekly, 26 September 1986, 91.
————. 17 July 1972, 122.

The Boy Who Reversed Himself
Belden, Elizabeth A., and Judith M. Beckman. *English Journal,* April
     1989, 89.
Book Report, May 1987, 38.
Burns, Mary M. *Horn Book,* January 1987, 62.

Cart, Michael. *School Library Journal,* November 1986, 108.

Children's Book Review Service, February 1987, 79.

Epstein, Connie C. *Horn Book,* November 1987, 777.

Hearne, Betsy. *Bulletin of the Center for Children's Books,* January 1987, 98.

Journal of Reading, November 1988, 102.

Kirkus Reviews, 1 October 1986, 1520.

Neumeyer, Peter. *New York Times Book Review,* 1 February 1987, 29.

Philip, Neil. *Times Educational Supplement,* 18 November 1988, 26.

Publishers Weekly, 28 November 1986, 76.

Rochman, Hazel. *Booklist,* 15 October 1986, 346.

Voice of Youth Advocates, June 1987, 93.

The Duplicate

Book Watch, August 1988, 7.

Children's Book Review Service, May 1988, 114.

Flowers, Ann A. *Horn Book,* May 1988, 362.

Harding, Susan M. *School Library Journal,* April 1988, 113.

Kirkus Reviews, 15 March 1988, 459.

Marcus, Leonard. *New York Times Book Review,* 27 November 1988, 36.

Roback, Diane, *Publishers Weekly,* 12 February 1988, 88.

Shelton, Helen H. *Childhood Education,* Spring 1989, 178.

Sutherland, Zena. *Bulletin of the Center for Children's Books,* April 1988, 168.

Voice of Youth Advocates, December 1988, 248.

Zvirin, Stephanie. *Booklist,* 15 May 1988, 1597.

Fingers

Best Sellers, December 1983, 350.

Book Report, March 1988, 39.

Bulletin of the Center for Children's Books, December 1983, 78.

Children's Book Review Service, December 1983, 44.

Daggett, Margaret L. English Journal, March 1987, 93.

Fantasy Review, August 1984, 51.

Kirkus Reviews, 1 November 1983, 208.

Jobe, Ronald A. *Language Arts,* January 1984, 69.

Magazine of Fantasy and Science Fiction, October 1988, 22.

Publishers Weekly, 5 July 1985, 68.

Twichell, Ethel R. *Horn Book,* December 1983, 719.

———. *Horn Book,* July 1987, 495.

Voice of Youth Advocates, April 1984, 35.

Wilson, Anita C. *School Library Journal,* October 1983, 173.

The Green Futures of Tycho
Bulletin of the Center for Children's Books, November 1981, 58.
Children's Book Review Service, March 1981, 69.
Cianciolo, Patricia J. *Reading Teacher,* March 1982, 752.
Daggett, Margaret L. *English Journal,* March 1987, 93.
Elleman, Barbara. *Booklist,* 1 April 1981, 1108.
Hamilton, Virginia. *New York Times Book Review,* 26 April 1981, 60.
Heins, Paul. *Horn Book,* August 1981, 426.
Hunter, C. Bruce. *Curriculum Review,* May 1985, 93.
Kirkus Reviews, 15 June 1981, 740.
Kliatt Young Adult Paperback Book Guide, Fall 1984, 30.
Learning: Creative Ideas and Insights for Teachers, April 1989, 66.
Magazine of Fantasy and Science Fiction, October 1988, 22.
Philip, Neil. *Times Educational Supplement,* 18 November 1988, 26.
Pollack, Pamela D. *School Library Journal,* April 1981, 133.
Stein, Ruth M. *Language Arts,* January 1982, 58.
Voice of Youth Advocates, October 1981, 45.

House of Stairs
Booklist, 1 June 1974, 1101.
———. 15 March 1975, 748.
Brotman, Sonia. *School Library Journal,* December 1976, 31.
Bulletin of the Center for Children's Books, November 1974, 53.
Carlson, G. Robert, Tony Manna, and Jan Yoder. *English Journal,* January 1976, 96.
Daggett, Margaret L. *English Journal,* March 1987, 93.
Emergency Librarian, January 1982, 18.
Heins, Peter. *Horn Book,* August 1974, 386.
Journal of Reading, November 1978, 128.
Kirkus Reviews, 15 April 1974, 434.
———. 1 January 1975, 11.
Library Journal, 15 May 1974, 1451.
———. 15 December 1974, 3248.
Philip, Neil. *Times Educational Supplement,* 18 November 1988, 26.
Pollack, Pamela D. *Library Journal,* 15 March 1974, 904.
Publishers Weekly, 6 May 1974, 68.
Rochman, Hazel. *School Library Journal,* October 1988, 39.
Sutton, Roger. *Horn Book,* May 1987, 368.
Weher, Rosemary, *Choice,* November 1975, 1133.

Interstellar Pig
Book Report, November 1986, 35.
Bulletin of the Center for Children's Books, July 1984, 213.

Byard, Rosalie. *New York Times Book Review,* 23 September 1984, 47.
Children's Book Review Service, August 1984, 154.
Daggett, Margaret L. *English Journal,* March 1987, 93.
Draper, Charlotte W. *Horn Book,* September 1984, 599.
———. *Horn Book,* March 1987, 235.
Elles, Sally., *Booklist,* 1 June 1984, 1392.
English Journal, December 1985, 49.
Fantasy Review, January 1985, 49.
———. April 1986, 31.
Jones, Trev. *School Library Journal,* September 1984, 134.
Junior Bookshelf, June 1987, 137.
Kirkus Reviews, 1 May 1984, 550.
Laski, Audrey. *Times Educational Supplement,* 29 July 1988, 21.
Nelms, Beth, and Ben Nelms. *English Journal,* April 1985, 83.
Publishers Weekly, 25 May 1984, 59.
———. 25 April 1986, 88.
School Librarian, May 1987, 159.
Science Fiction Review, August 1986, 33.
Tomasetti, Camille A. *Best Sellers,* October 1984, 279.
Voice of Youth Advocates, April 1985, 57.

Into the Dream

Bulletin of the Center for Children's Books, December 1979, 82.
Children's Book Review Service, March 1979, 79.
Churchman, Deborah. *Christian Science Monitor,* 6 July 1984, B4.
Elleman, Barbara. *Booklist,* 15 February 1979, 936.
Kirkus Reviews, 1 March 1979, 263.
Pollack, Pamela D. *School Library Journal,* January 1979, 57.
Reading Teacher, October 1980, 53.
Roedder, Kathleen R. *Childhood Education,* April/May 1980, 306.
Stein, Ruth M. *Language Arts,* February 1980, 189.
Yeager, Allan. *Instructor,* November 1979, 140.

Once, Said Darlene

Babbling Bookworm, October 1979, 4.
Bulletin of the Center for Children's Books, October 1979, 38.
Children's Book Review Service, May 1979, 95.
Coffey, Kathy. *School Library Journal,* May 1979, 78.
Goldberger, Judith. *Booklist,* 15 May 1979, 1445.
Kirkus Reviews, 1 March 1979, 262.
Publishers Weekly, 12 March 1979, 77.

Run
Journal of Reading, November 1978, 127.
Kirkus Reviews, 1 April 1973, 397.
Library Journal, 15 November 1973, 3457.

Singularity
Bartkiewicz, Ann. *Best Seller,* August 1985, 199.
Bulletin of the Center for Children's Books, June 1985, 195.
Children's Book Review Service, June 1985, 123.
Daggett, Margaret L. *English Journal,* March 1987, 93.
English Journal, December 1986, 61.
Fantasy Review, December 1986, 41.
Flowers, Ann A. *Horn Book,* May 1985, 320.
Gale, David. *School Library Journal,* August 1985, 82.
Kirkus Reviews, 1 March 1985, J19.
Nelms, Beth, and Ben Nelms. *English Journal,* February 1986, 106.
Philip, Neil. *Times Educational Supplement,* 18 November 1988, 26.
Publishers Weekly, 26 April 1985, 82.
Science Fiction Chronicle, December 1986, 46.
Science Fiction Review, August 1985, 19.
Turner, Ann. *Childhood Education,* May 1986, 372.
Voice of Youth Advocates, October 1985, 270.
Zvirin, Stephanie. *Booklist,* 1 April 1985, 1114.

Strange Attractors
Burns, Mary M. *Horn Book,* March/April 1990, 210.
Cart, Michael. *School Library Journal,* December 1989, 120.
MacRae, Cathi. *Wilson Library Bulletin,* November 1989, 97.

That's Silly
Booklist, 15 June 1981, 1350.
Bulletin of the Center for Children's Books, September 1981, 17.
Kirkus Reviews, 15 June 1981, 738.
Palmer, Nancy. *School Library Journal,* February 1982, 71.

Index

The Authors

James E. Davis, professor of English at Ohio University in Athens, is president-elect of the National Council of Teachers of English (NCTE). He reviews regularly for the *ALAN Review* and frequently contributes to the journals of NCTE and its affiliates. He has edited the *Ohio English Bulletin, FOCUS,* and the book *Dealing with Censorship.*

Hazel K. Davis, teacher of English and reading at Federal Hocking High School, Stewart, Ohio, has been president of NCTE's Assembly on Literature for Adolescents (ALAN) and the Ohio Council of Teachers of English Language Arts. She is a reviewer for *ALAN Review, FOCUS,* and often speaks and writes on literature for young adults.

James and Hazel Davis are co-editors of the 1988 edition of *Your Reading,* the junior high/middle school booklist for NCTE.

The Editor

Patricia J. Campbell has taught adolescent literature at UCLA and is the former assistant coordinator of young adult services at the Los Angeles Public Library. From 1978 to 1988 she reviewed young adult books in a monthly column for the *Wilson Library Bulletin,* for which she now writes a monthly review column on the independent press. Her five books include *Presenting Robert Cormier,* the first volume in Twayne's Young Adult Author Series. In 1989 she received the American Library Association Grolier Award for distinguished achievement with young people and books. She and her husband, David Shore, write and publish books on overseas campervan travel.